USING YOUR HOME OVEN

MAKE YOUR OWN

Belt Buckles
Necklaces
Earrings
Beads
Bolos
Pins
Buttons
Barrettes

Using the easy-to-work-with modeling compound many of today's top jewelry designers use.

by Betty Foster

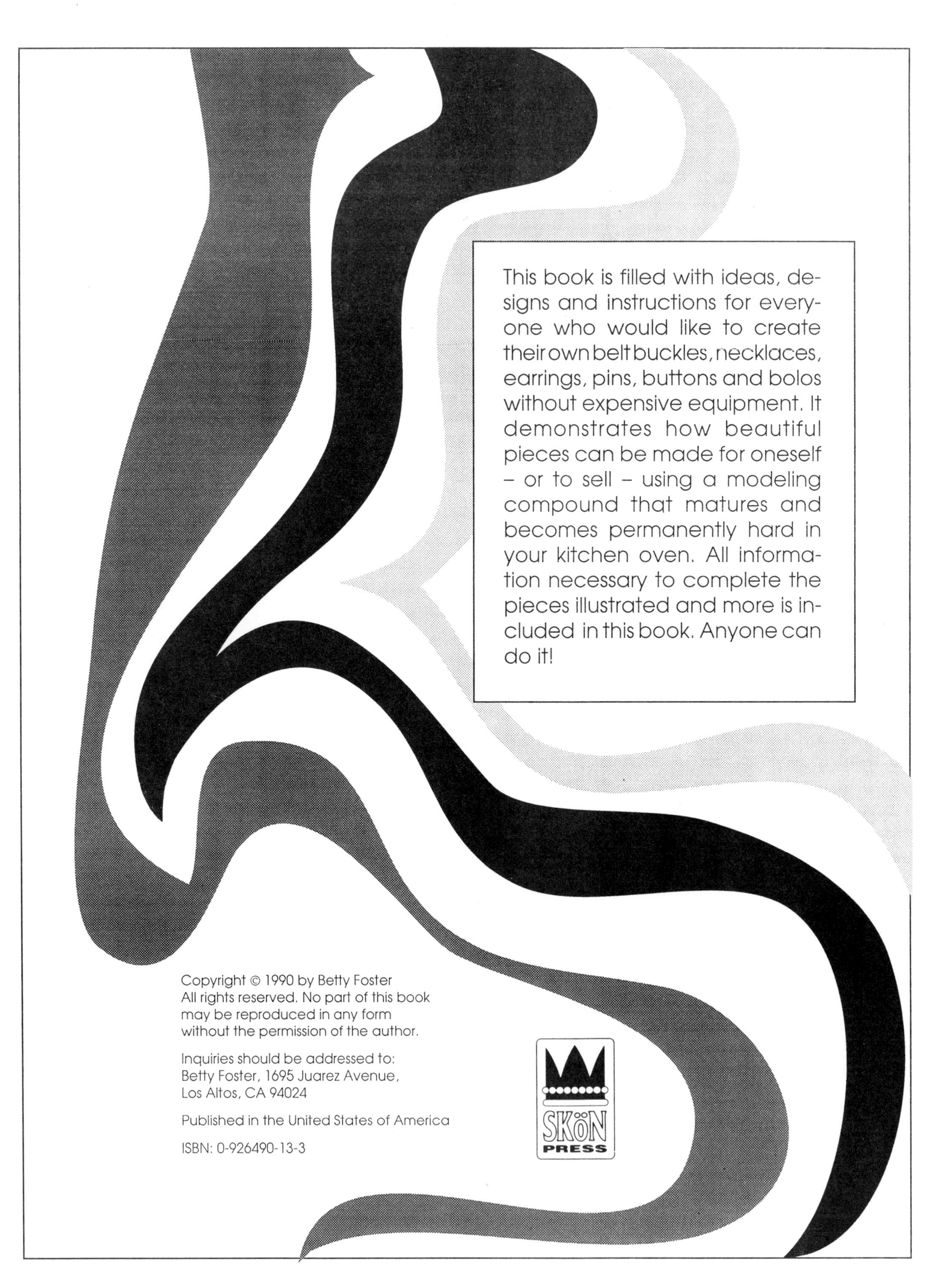

This book is filled with ideas, designs and instructions for everyone who would like to create their own belt buckles, necklaces, earrings, pins, buttons and bolos without expensive equipment. It demonstrates how beautiful pieces can be made for oneself – or to sell – using a modeling compound that matures and becomes permanently hard in your kitchen oven. All information necessary to complete the pieces illustrated and more is included in this book. Anyone can do it!

Inquiries should be addressed to:
Betty Foster, 1695 Juarez Avenue,
Los Altos, CA 94024

Published in the United States of America

ISBN: 0-926490-13-3

SKöN PRESS

PIN FOR
SCARF ON
PAGE 56
YOU'LL FIND
THIS NECKLACE
ON PAGE 70
ABSTRACT
BUCKLE ON PAGE 39
NECKLACE AND
MATCHING EARRINGS
FROM PAGE 59

CONTENTS

INTRODUCTION

Sterling silver, gold, porcelain, stoneware clay, leather and wooden handmade buckles and jewelry have been around for a very long time. Recently, however, jewelry, accessories and many other items have been appearing throughout the country in boutiques and gift shops made from a modeling compound that is by no means new, but has just recently started to reach it's potential. Designs made from this material have been priced at $30.00 and up – putting it in a class with other fine handmade jewelry.

This material has been referred to as low-fired clay. Although it does not have the properties such as earth or mud, it does have the same modeling capabilities as regular clay – so calling it low-fired clay isn't stretching it too far. Throughout this book the word "firing" will be used instead of "baking".

One of the great advantages of using this material is that it is fired in your own kitchen oven from 250° F to 325° F for only 15 to 25 minutes. After firing it is hard, but maintains some flexibility, making it virtually unbreakable. As with all firings of clay, etc., care should be taken to have good ventilation in the room.

The color range of this compound is so wide that any color can be achieved by simply mixing and kneading. It also comes in translucent, pearlized and metallic colors. Bulk or mixed colors in 2-ounce pieces in a box may be purchased. The fact that it is so clean to work with should appeal to anyone who sews and wishes to make belt buckles, jewelry or other accessories to go with a particular outfit. Another advantage: you can be interrupted in the middle of a project and leave it without worrying about it drying out. Also, because of its lack of shrinkage it can be made in the exact size and shape you want it to be. Besides the big advantage of not requiring a large expensive kiln for firing, very few tools are needed. The tools required can usually be found around your home.

There are several different brands of modeling compound. The two brands the artists have used throughout this book are Sculpey III and Fimo. Fimo's colors are a bit more intense than Sculpey III, But there is also a Super Sculpey that is just a buff color that is used in some unusual ways in this book. They are readily available at your local craft shop or from the sources listed in the back of this book. Call or write for their catalogs. These will feature glazes and other items you will want to use with these compounds.

In this book we have presented many different ways this modeling compound may be used to make any accessories you desire. As you begin working and creating the designs illustrated you will discover your own ideas unfolding. There are endless ways of using it and we wish you joy in discovering them.

BASIC TOOLS AND STEPS

All items listed may be found in your own home, at your local craft shop and at shops listed in the **SOURCES** section on page 88

Below is a list of ***Basic Tools and Materials*** for working with this modeling compound:

1. Modeling compound in colors or amounts needed for your designs. Always good to have more.
2. Small rolling pin or plastic or wooden dowl for rolling out the material.
3. A small sharp knife. A kitchen knife or one used for clay work is good.
4. Wooden tools. A flat popsicle stick and a wooden pointer (such as a pencil) for making holes.

5. Clear gloss or matte lacquer spray if you want a glazed look. (See **PRODUCTS** page 86).
6. Glue (See **PRODUCTS** page 86).
7. Roll of wax paper or plain white paper (like typing or loose leaf paper). This is for rolling clay between – enabling you to use a fresh sheet each time you use a different color, thereby preventing picking up another color.
8. Cookie sheet or any flat baking pan for firing pieces.
9. Buckle, pin, earring, button, bolo or necklace fasteners (see **FASTENERS** page 82).
10. Extruder

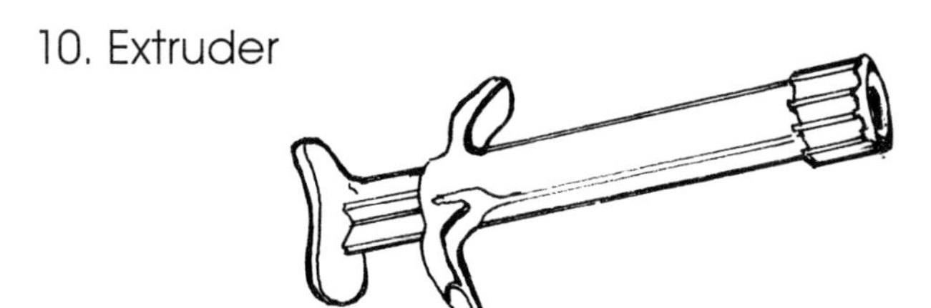

BASIC TOOLS AND STEPS, continued

11. Cord for stringing beads or hanging a pendant.
12. Tape applicator (see below) if you want to hem your belts as described in section **MAKING BELTS** page 22).

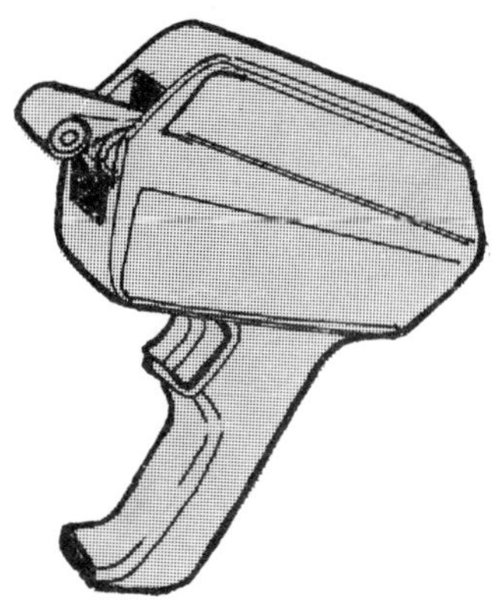

13. Tool for putting beads on for spraying or glazing (see how to make on page 18).
14. Plastic disk to fit your hand or a block of wood for pressing

---

SOFTENING THE MODELING COMPOUND

The following illustrations will tell you an easy way to do this:

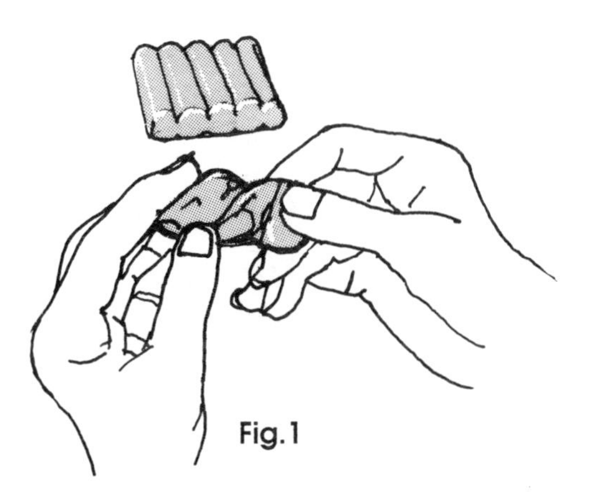

Fig.1

Start with a piece about 1/2 the size of a two-ounce piece. Twist with your fingers as shown. **(Fig.1)**

After doing this, put it in the palms of your hands and roll it back and forth, then flatten it a few times – this will further soften it. If you need more than this amount, keep adding to it in the same way. **(Fig.2)**

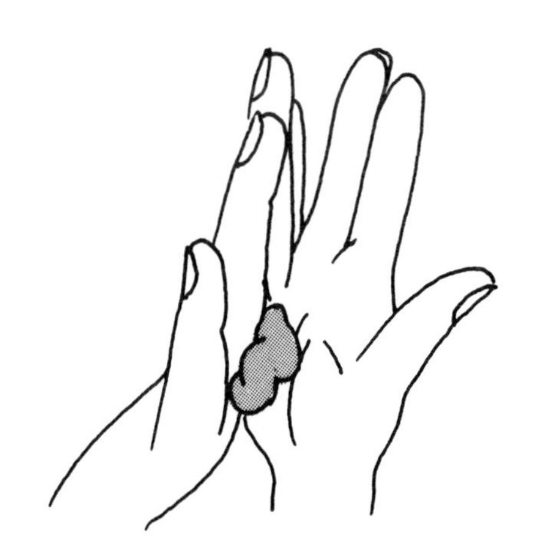

Fig.2

Softening the Modeling Compound, continued

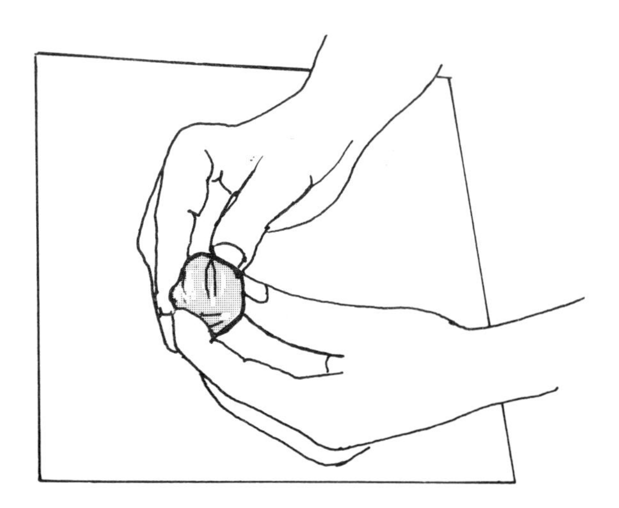

When it is pliable proceed with the method you will use for the certain design you intend to create. If it requires rolling out to cut a design from it first roll the material into a ball then flatten it with your fingers **(Fig. 3)**

Fig.3

The easiest – and cleanest – way to roll your piece is to place it between two pieces of wax paper (or plain paper) **(Fig.4)**. This way you can use fresh paper for each color you intend to use. Also your rolling pin or wooden dowel does not pick up the color. Keep a bottle of hand lotion and a towel nearby to clean your hands off after each color. The hand lotion on your hand will even help with softening the compound.

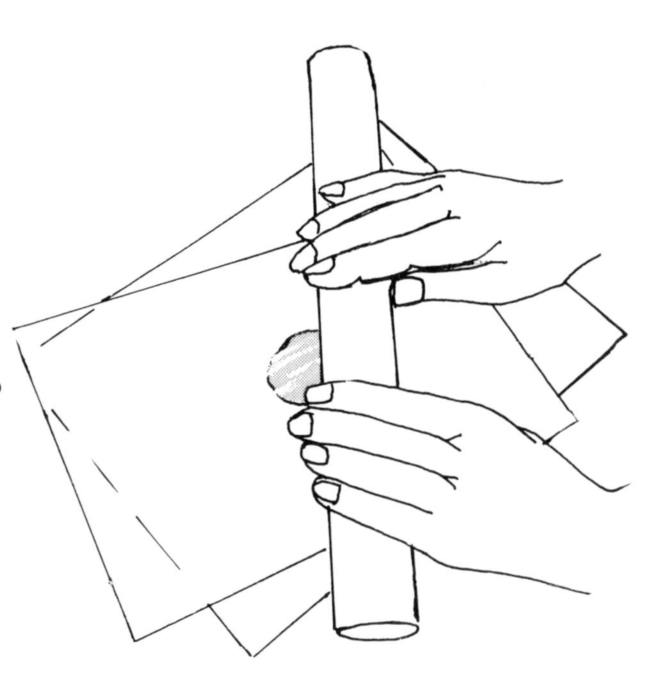

Fig.4

BASIC STEPS, continued

A few helpful hints:

1. Get a box of sandwich bags to keep mixed pieces or left over pieces in to keep them separate. Also use them to keep pieces you have removed from their original wrapping.
2. Remember no material is ever wasted. Small pieces can be used to make buttons, pins or magnets.
3. If after firing a flat piece you have rolled you discover a few bumps (like bubbles), you simply have to take a piece of medium fine sandpaper and sand it down. It is best to sand in one direction. This does not change the color or design in any way. If you want to make a lined design on a plain piece, take a very rough piece of sand paper and rub in one direction several times. You can then rub a buff stain on this to achieve a wood-grain effect.

COLOR

The wide range of colors that are available in modeling compounds is discussed in the introduction. Below are a few suggestions of color combination to give you a start on blending colors to reach certain shades and values.

Dark green	green/small piece of black
Lime green	green/small piece of white
Olive green	yellow/small piece of green
Dark olive	orange/small piece of black
Blue green	blue/small piece of yellow
Golden yellow	yellow/small piece of orange
Soft brown	brown/small piece of orange
Wine	red/small piece of black
Violet	blue/small piece of red, small piece of black
Light violet	blue/small piece of red, small piece of white

COLOR, continued

You will soon come up with color combinations of your own. To match or blend with an outfit you may be making, keep experimenting with little pieces of this compound until you get the color you need.

To achieve these colors and any other combinations use a larger piece of the main color, soften it and roll it into a thick roll. Do the same with the other colors you wish to mix. Then twist them together, flatten and knead them until you get the color you want. In order to get the desired shade you may have to add a bit of one color or more. After experimenting a few times you will see how many beautiful colors and shades you can make. Remember always that black will darken and white will lighten. It is a lot like mixing paints. The color resulting from the blending will be the same after firing. Only red and yellow darken a bit after firing – so fire these a bit lower.

There are many ways this compound may be textured. (see **TEXTURING** page 17). Glass, wood, wire, metallic thread or any semi-precious stone may be imbedded in it. These may be fired in it and then a clear glaze put over it to secure them.

The designs of the three artists represented in this book are made in several different ways. Some have used only the colors of the modeling compound itself. Another has used her secret way of coloring the neutral shades of the compound. Some are made by painting with acrylics. They are all explained in detail as we go along so it will be easy to follow the directions.

MARBLEIZING AND OTHER DESIGN METHODS

To get a marbleized effect, roll two or more colors into thin tubes. Lay them together and twist like a candy cane. **(Fig.5).**

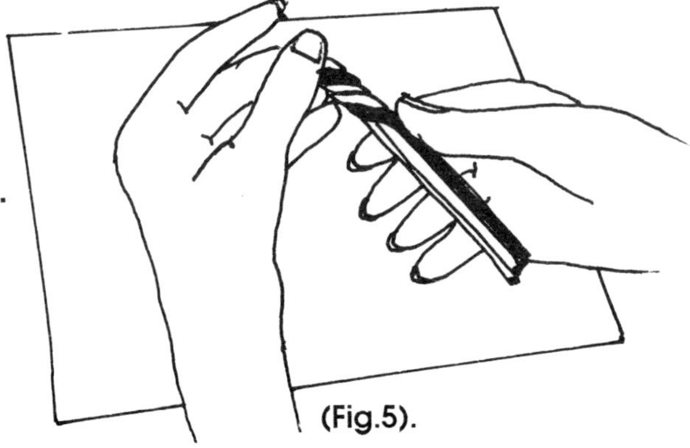

(Fig.5).

MARBLEIZING AND OTHER DESIGN METHODS, continued

Press the cane together. **Fig.6.** Place on a piece of wax paper, with another piece of wax paper(or just plain paper) on top of it. Roll it out. When cutting a design from this, place the pattern you decide to use on the most interesting part of the piece. (remember what is left over can be used for another pattern or made into beads).

Fig.6

You may also roll out several thin pieces of different colors and place them on top of one another – then roll them up. **Fig.7.** Put this in the refrigerator (or freezer) to firm up a bit , then cut into slices. These can be used for bolos, pins of magnets, or – with a hole in them – used for a necklace.

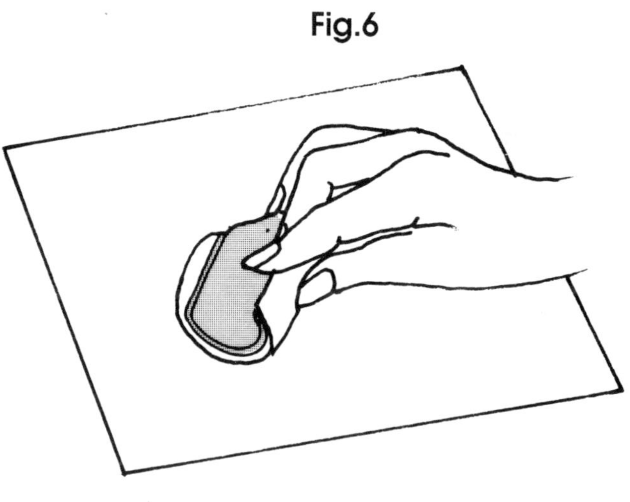

Fig.7

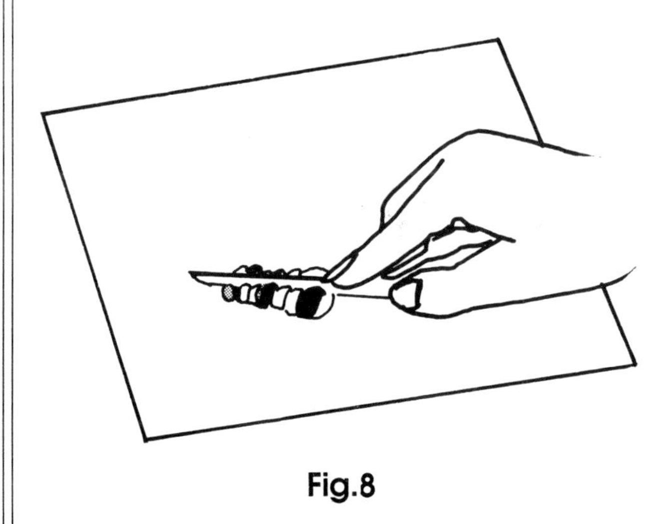

Fig.8

To make a different marbleized effect roll the colors into thick tubes and twist into a cane. Then, instead of flattening it, cut it lengthwise into two pieces. Place them side-by-side and roll out. You will get an entirely different effect doing this. The surprises you get from the different treatments of this material is part of the fun of working with it. **Fig.8.**

FLOWER DESIGNS

To make simple flower designs roll one color (a dark one) into about a 1/4" diameter tube. Then roll another color into seven thinner tubes. Place the seven tubes around the one dark tube. **(Fig.9)**

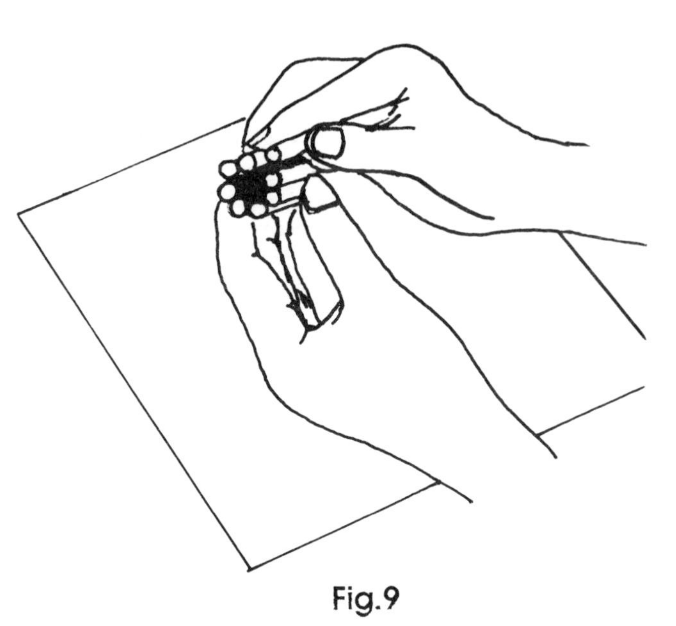

Fig.9

Roll out a third color – rather thin – and roll it around the eight tubes. **(Fig.10)**

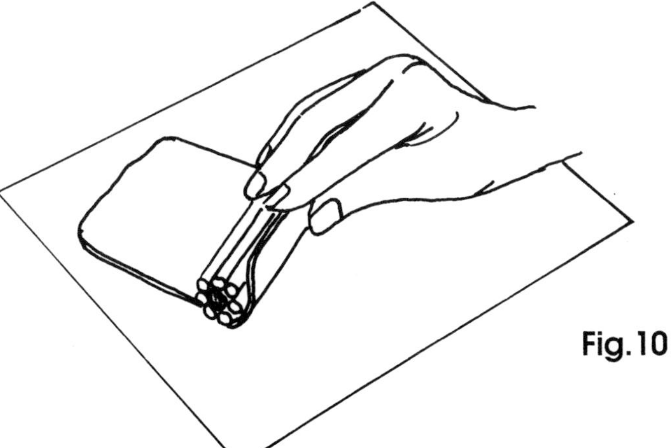

Fig.10

When firmed up a bit, cut with **EXACTO** knife and you will see the "flower" design **(Fig.11).**

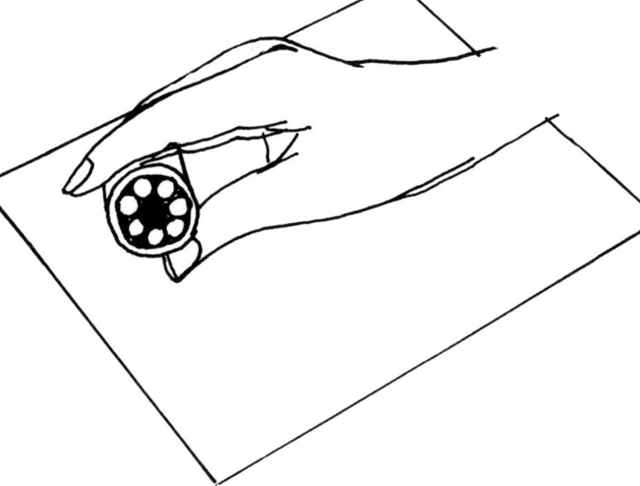

Fig.11

TEXTURING

Some of the best sources for texturing surfaces are old India wood blocks that are used for printing on fabrics. Small pressing molds may be made from these by taking a roll of the compound and pressing the end of it into a certain section of the wood block, then firing it in your oven. You may reverse the design by pressing the part you have just finished firing into another roll of the compound. You will then have two different interesting effects.

Your own designs may be made by filling paper cups with plaster (using a formula of 2 1/2 to 3 pounds of plaster to a quart of water). When they are firm – but not completely dry – scratch your own design into them with a pointed tool. It is best to draw your design on paper first. You now have some textured compound molds that can be used repeatedly in different ways.

Some of the most unusual things make interesting textures on the compound. The soles of some old walking shoes once made a terrific texture on one of my belt buckles. For example: ends of a spool of thread, rough sandpaper, combs, unusual rocks, shells, starfish, rings, burlap, string, screening, ends of keys, paper doilies, lace, etc. The list is endless. Don't forget things you see on walks – dried dill, hollow plant stems, dried flowers, ferns, leaves. One of the most popular belts was made by rolling the stem of a magnolia blossom around the edge. Even cloud formations and footprints have suggested new shapes.

Have fun observing everything wherever you go. All designs and shapes have already been made by the Master Designer. Become aware of them and become part of the universe.

Firing and Glazing

Throughout this book the word "firing" will be used for "baking"

Firing

When firing, put larger and thicker pieces together for one firing, beads and smaller pieces together for another firing. This is because you should not fire the thinner, smaller ones quite as long – or as hot– as the larger ones. Also the yellow and red colors darken a bit if fired too long. Firing range is from 250° to 325° for 15 to 20 minutes. After you do a few pieces you will be able to gauge the time and temperature according to your oven.

Glazing

If you like the rich satin look the pieces have with no glaze on them you may just leave them as they are. However, a thin matt glaze sprayed on them will enhance their look. If you prefer a shiny finish use a semi-gloss or gloss acrylic spray. There are many brands available at your local craft shops. When you spray, do it outdoors if possible or be sure to have proper ventilation in the room. Follow directions on the can. When spraying or brushing glaze on flat pieces elevate them a bit by putting a small piece of the compound under them so they do not stick to the surface. (See **PRODUCTS** page 86 for suggested spray glazes)

Spraying beads

Use a piece of wood about 18" long and 1 1/2" to 2" wide. Any piece of molding will do. Put a long nail in each end. Tie a piece of cord (one your beads can slide on) at one end.

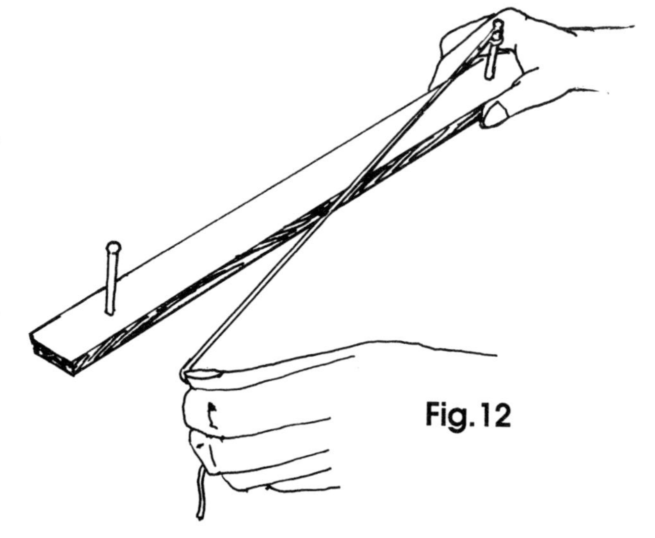

Fig.12

Spraying Beads, continued

Slide the beads onto it then secure at the other end **(Fig. 13).** Wrap a rubber band around the opposite nail before you tie it, then you will not have to knot it but only tie it once. Be sure there is space left between the beads so they will not stick together. Spray one side lightly, turn bead holder around and spray the other side. Let dry. Do this at least twice. Before removing, check to see that there are no spots not covered. If there are, just spray that area again.

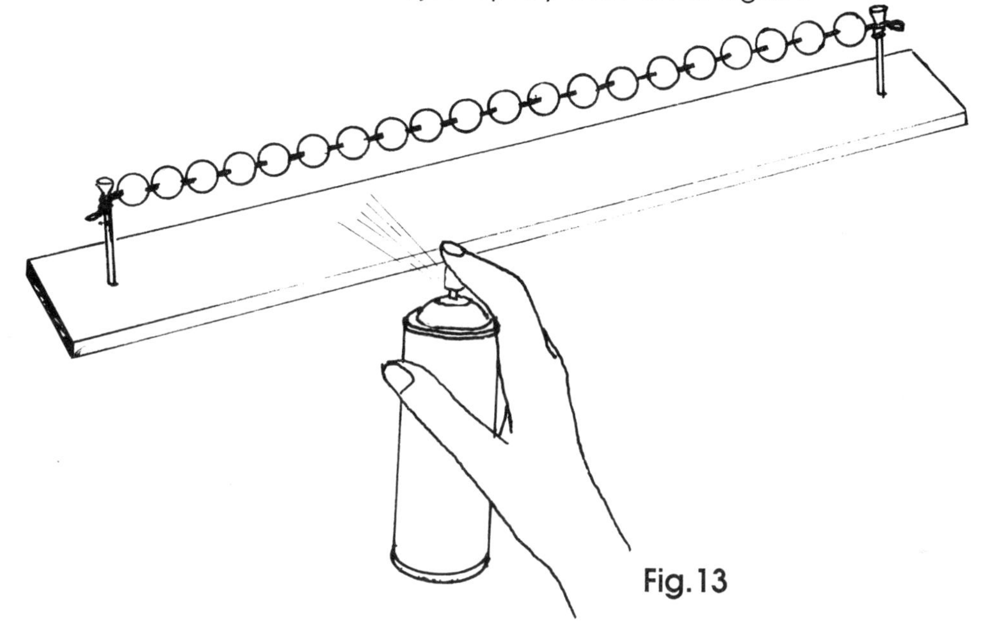

Fig. 13

Brush Glazing

If you want to use a glaze that must be applied with a brush place the beads on a piece of paper. Hold one with a pencil or pointed tool and brush glaze one half of the bead **(Fig. 14).** Let dry, then turn it over and do the same to the other side.

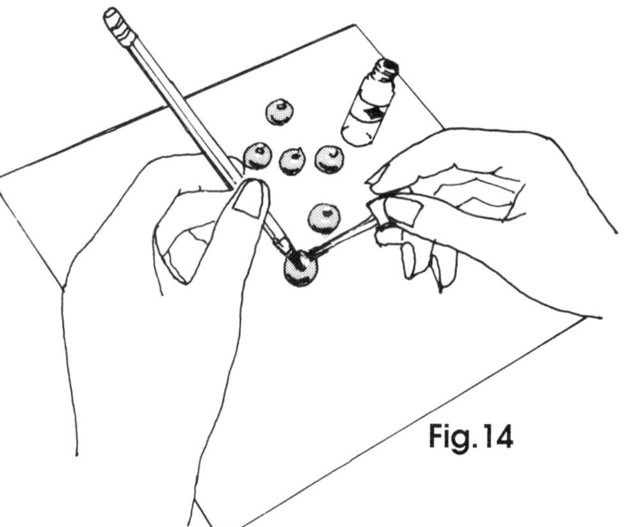

Fig. 14

Belt Buckles

MAKING BELTS

Since belts are a very important fashion accessory it is a good idea to spend a little time considering the different types that you can make.

The stretch belt seems to be the most popular. It is available in many different colors in either a knit stretch or a gabardine stretch. Sources listed in the back of the book tell you where you may purchase these. Your local fabric shop also carries a nice selection now, as handmade belts are becoming more popular.

Non stretch belts like the one used with Buckle B5 can be made in several different ways. Pigsuede, leather or ultra suede may be used hemmed or with no hem without an interfacing. Cut the material at least 6" longer than your waist for pulling through the loops to adjust.If it is to be hemmed cut it 1" wider than you want the finished belt to be. Taper it as in illustration. This makes it easier to slip through the buckle openings.

To hem the sides turn them back 1/2" on each side. Then stitch on a sewing machine – or you may use a **Scotch ATG** applicator equipped with two-sided sticky tape (See **BASIC TOOLS AND STEPS** for information). To use this applicator, you simply place the belt on a flat surface and holding one end roll the tape close to the edge down one side and then fold over (see sketches below). The tape is about 1" wide, so you will have a 1/2" hem. Repeat on the other side.

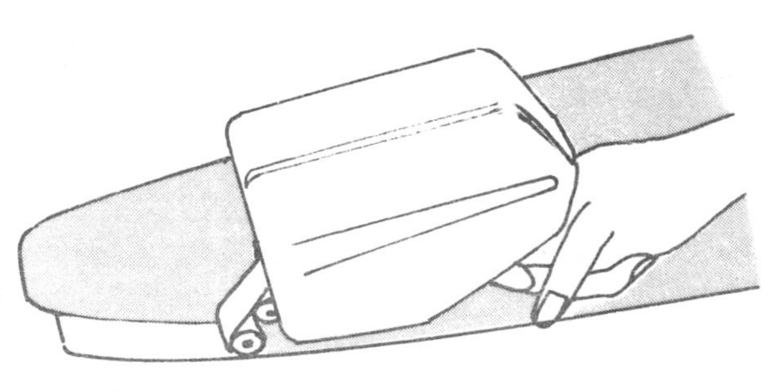

Fig.40

Fig.41

MAKING BELTS, continued

Another way to hem the sides is to use a leather or fabric glue or cement – either Barge Cement or Tandy Leather Cement work well. Follow directions on tube for applying.

Belts used with the adjustable fastener that is glued on the back of the buckle are finished in the same way, however, a belt eye is sewed on one end to fasten to the connector. The end that slides through the loop on the fastener is used to adjust the belt for fit (see illustration page 83).

Buckle B5 is a very nice buckle style you will want to use with your own fabric belt. You may use any color or design to complement the color or pattern of your outfit. When making belts from a thinner fabric it is best to interface them with buckrum or any stiffener. Everyone who does their own sewing will no doubt have their favorite method for making belts. If you want to make a belt out of the fabric your dress is made from make a plain buckle (see sketch below).

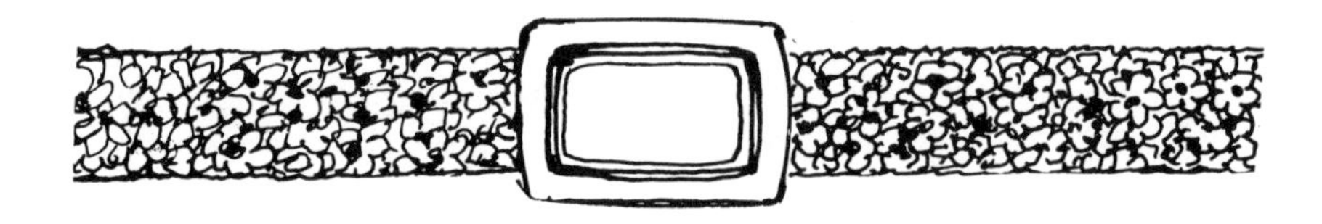

Use an adjustable belt fastener on the back. Sew a belt eye on one end.

When you want to match the belt to a printed fabric but use a plain belt, make a plain buckle and laminate on it a design cut from the fabric. Use one of the stretch belt fasteners for this.

It is even possible to use the stretch belt fasteners on a fabric belt you have made by fitting it exactly to your waist. By doing this you may even buy an inexpensive belt and remove the plain buckle and add an original buckle of your own. Now let's go on to making some buckles.

BUCKLE B1

This is one of the easiest methods for making a belt buckle in the book. It is simply extruding different colored tubes and pressing them on an oblong slab.

Colors used in this one are a metallic pewter for the oblong base and for the extruded pieces dark brown, chartreuse, bright green and black. It is on a 2" silver gray stretch belt.

THESE TWO DESIGNS ARE MADE
THE SAME AS B1. JUST PUT THE TUBES
IN A DIFFERENT DESIGN

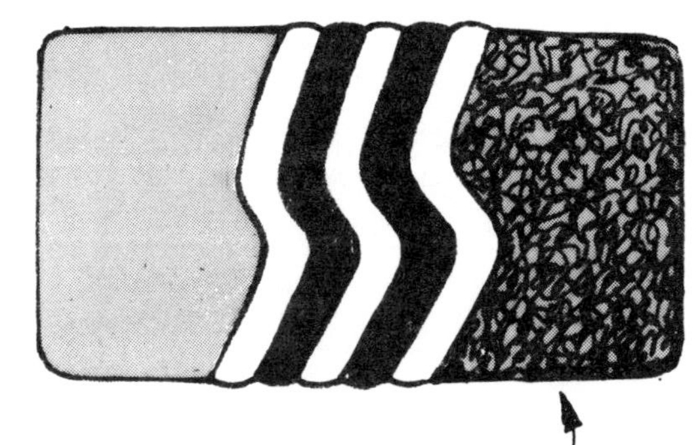

TEXTURE BACKGROUND FOR A
DIFFERENT EFFECT

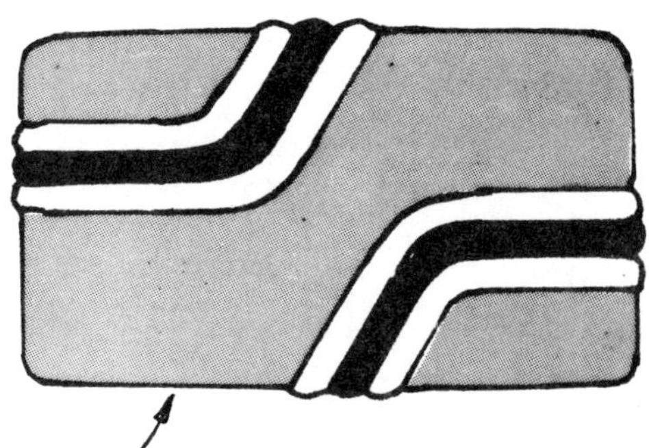

METALLIC IS NICE FOR THE
BACKGROUND - THEN SELECT
COLORS THAT MATCH AN OUTFIT

Buckle B1

1 two-ounce piece metallic pewter
3 rolls from 2 ounces of brown
2 rolls from 2 ounces of chartreuse
2 rolls from 2 ounces of bright green
2 rolls from 2 ounces of black

This is a very simple buckle and you may use any colors you wish. It can easily be matched to any clothes you want to use it with. Cut out the pattern from buckle and earring for your base color (This one is metallic pewter). Select 4 colors you wish to use and roll or press them through the extruder. If they are hard to put through the extruder, put a drop of oil into the channel. Also get the modeling material as soft as you can.

After cutting out the base apply the tubes **(Fig. 42).** When all are in place the top and the bottom edge should be equal. To fire make a tube 3" by about 1/2" X 1/4" to curve the buckle over to fit waist **(Fig. 43).**

(Fig. 42)

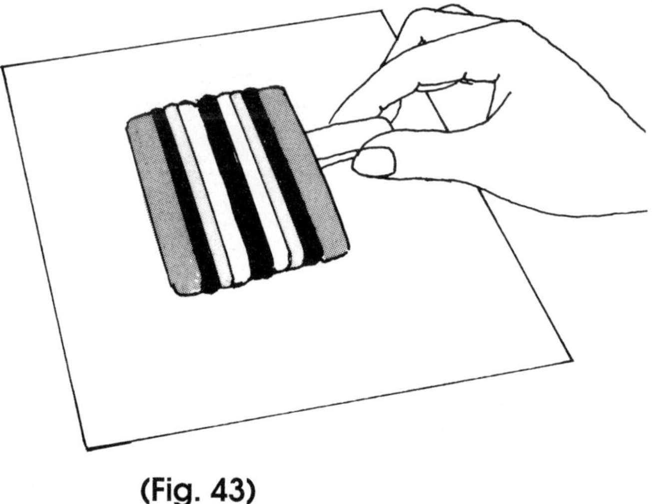

(Fig. 43)

Fire and glue a buckle fastener on back. Get one from a source listed on the **Source** page in the back of the book or from your fabric shop and attach to stretch belting. Glaze if you care to.

BUCKLE B2

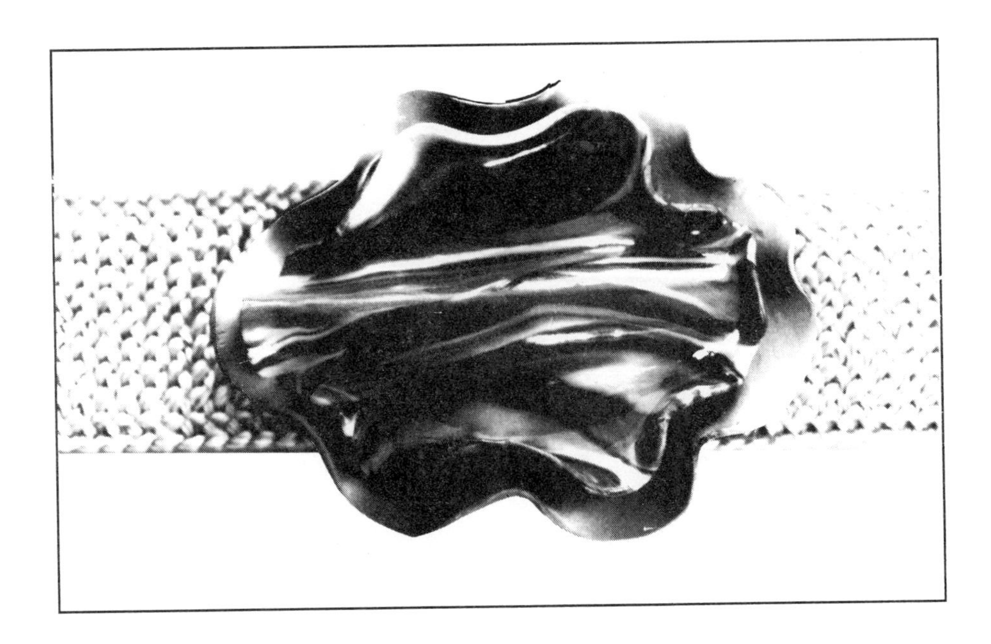

The background of this belt buckle is metallic copper. The center piece is orange, dark blue, metallic copper and metallic pewter. It is on a 2" stretch sand belt.

This is an abstract shape that can be made in many different ways.

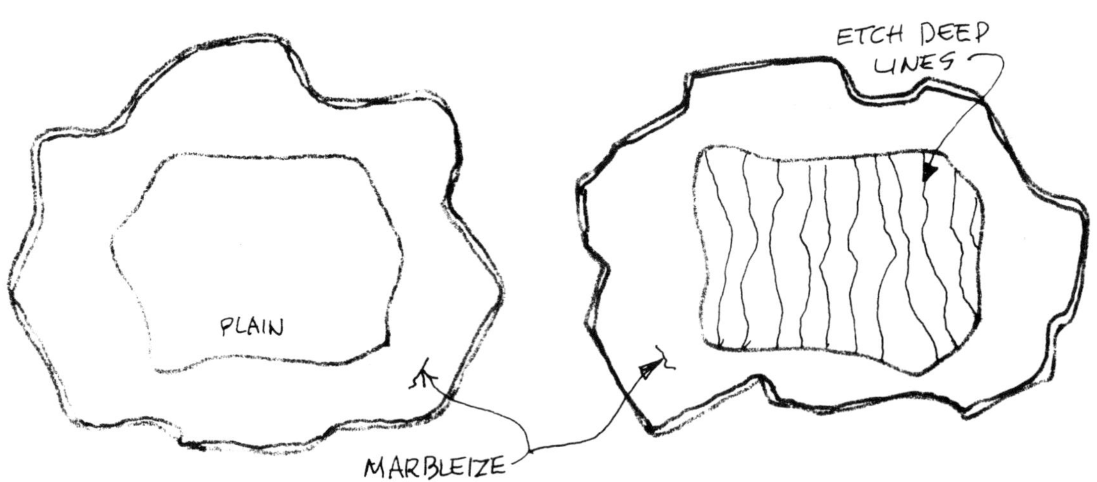

Buckle B2

1 two-ounce metallic copper (for part one)

Use the following for the marbleized piece (part two)

1 small roll of 2-ounce chartreuse
1 small roll of 2 ounce orange
1 small roll of 2-ounce blue
1 small roll of 2-ounce metallic copper
1 small roll of 2-ounce metallic pewter

The pattern for this can be used as is or as a guideline for any shape you wish to make. After you have your shape cut out from about a 1/8 inch slab, press the edges to make thinner **(Fig.44),** using a plaster bat or piece of wood.

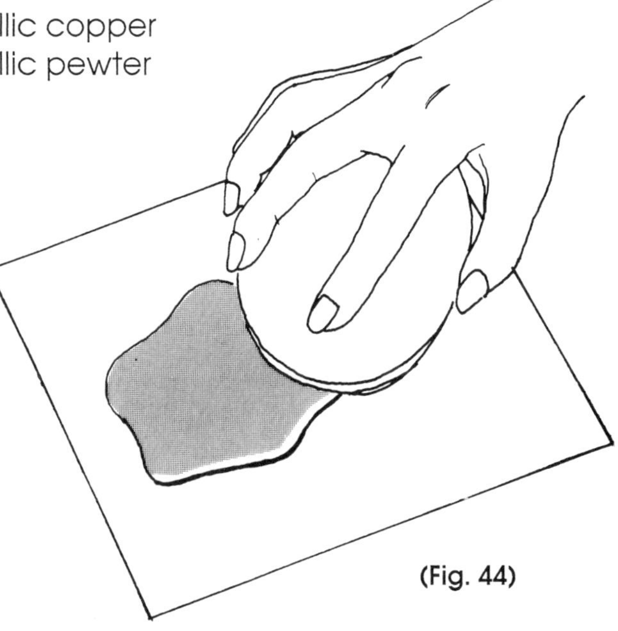

(Fig. 44)

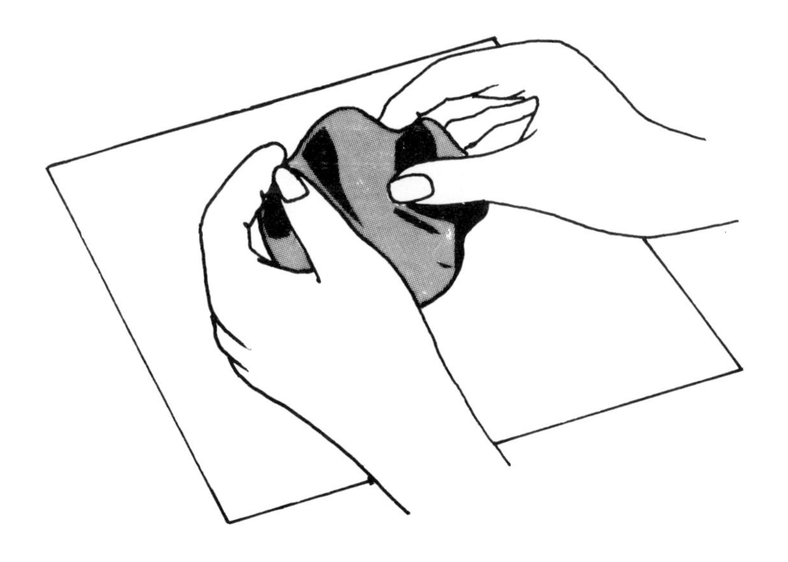

(Fig. 45)

Then ruffle the edges **(Fig.45)** - stretching as you go around, and pressing under or up. Make the ruffles any way that appeals to you.

Fire this before making inset piece (pattern - Part 2) Do the earrings with the inset on copper - or just plain copper - and ruffle the way you did Part 1 of the necklace. Stretch inside of the earring to dome it a bit.

Buckle B2, continued

To make the inset piece, roll the 5 colors (or colors of your choice) into tubes and twist it like a candy cane to make the marbleized piece as explained on page 14. Then roll it out and cut Part 2 pattern out and fit it into the fired base piece. You may have to cut it or stretch it a bit until you get it to fit, leaving about 1/4" of copper showing around the edges. Fire this right inside the already fired piece. This provides a nice fit. When it is fired, lift it out and glue it in. Glaze if you care to and glue belt fastener on back. Use any stretch belting you care to.

TWO MORE BELT BUCKLE IDEAS!

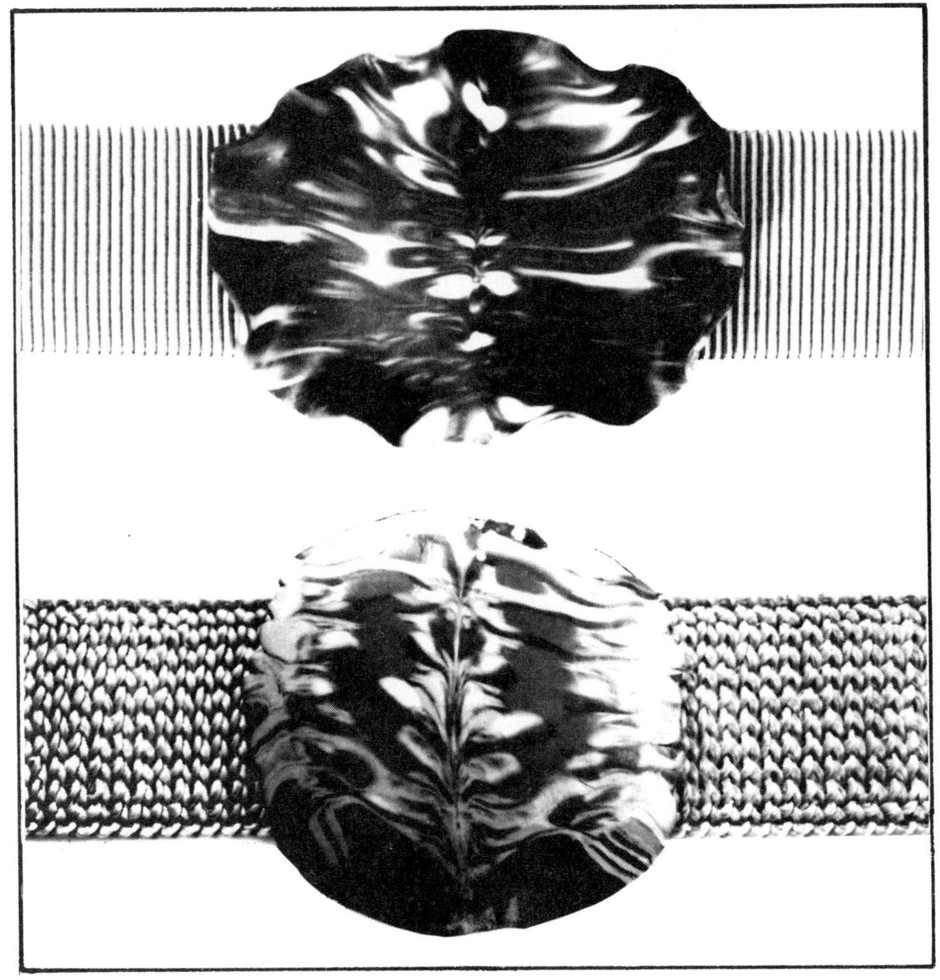

Buckle B3

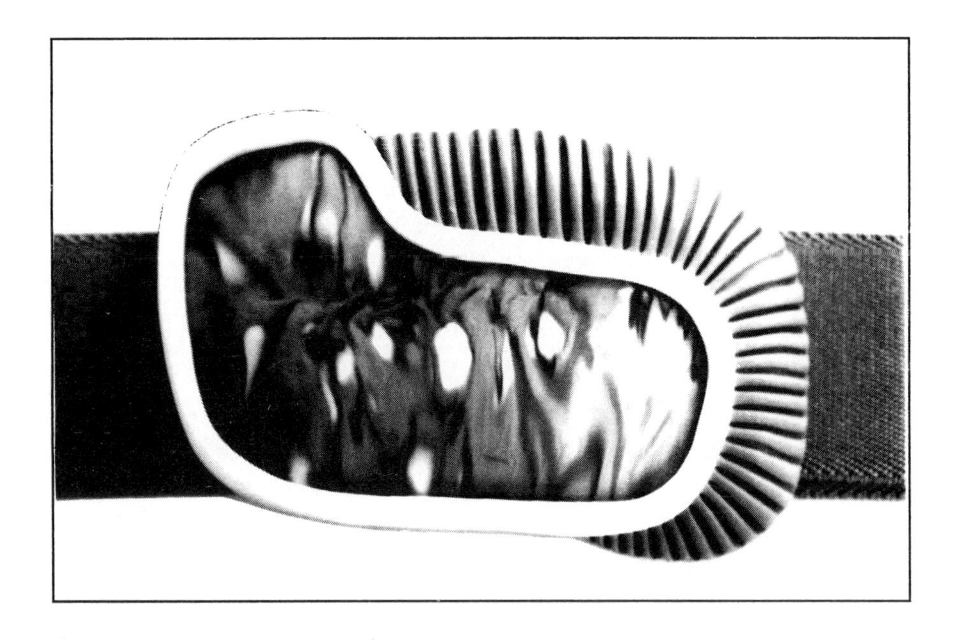

A royal blue gabardine stretch belt is used on this design. Blue, green and yellow comprise the marbelized part. Of course different colors can be used – or you could use Part 2 alone – but cutting it a little bigger.

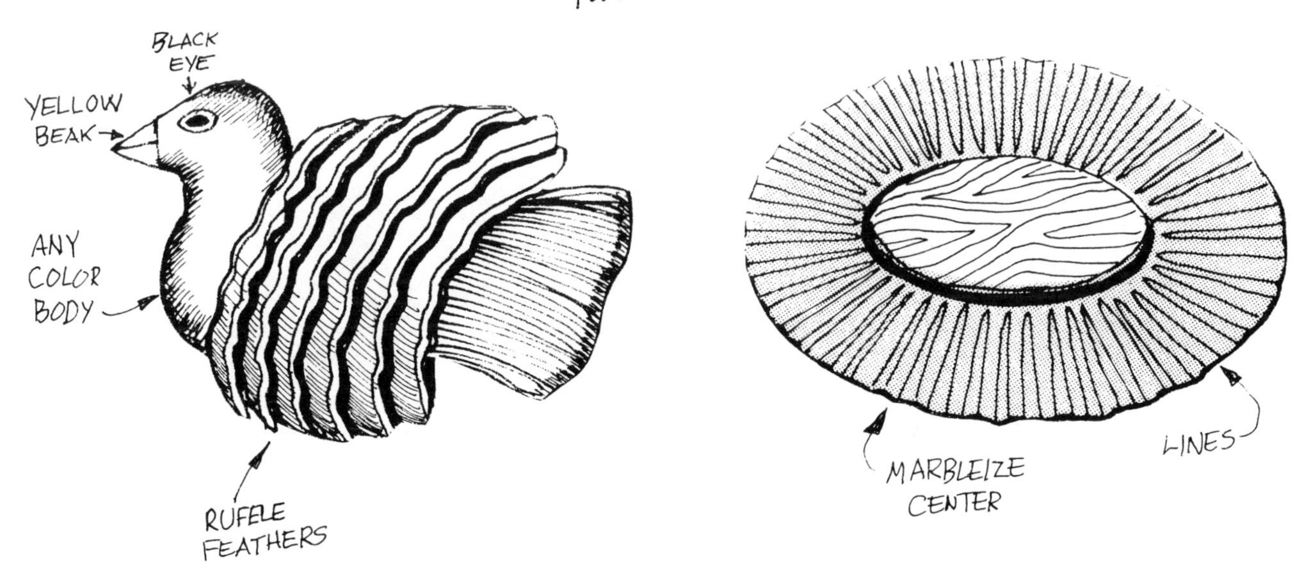

Buckle B3

Use one 2-ounce blue. Soften and roll it out and cut out using pattern Part 1. Put lines in it as shown. For Part 2 use two small rolls of the same blue, one small roll of green, one small roll of yellow. Follow directions for marbleizing on page 14 – where it describes how to twist all these into a candy cane texture. Cut through the middle and leave them side by side – then press them out. Cut out, using pattern Part 2.

Fit Part 2 onto Part 1, using the line on Part 1 as a guide **(Fig.46).** Press down, then soften two small rolls of yellow and press through the extruder – or roll into a tube by hand. Put around outside of Part 2. Press the seams together around the outside edge. Curve around waist to fit and place on a tube when you fire so that it remains curved. Fire and glaze – or leave it as is. Sometimes the silky look is nicer. Glue on fastener F2 for a stretch belt.

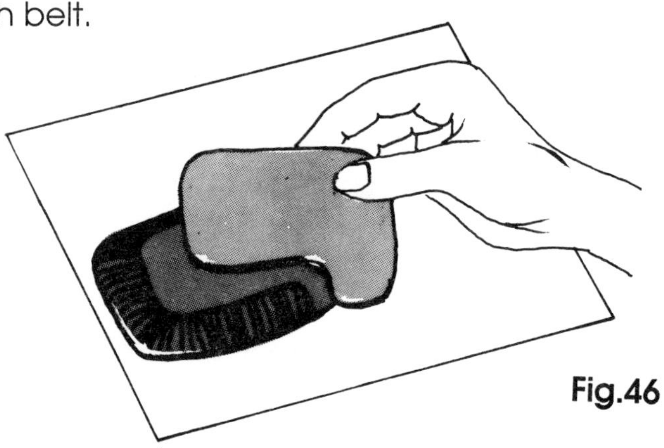

Fig.46

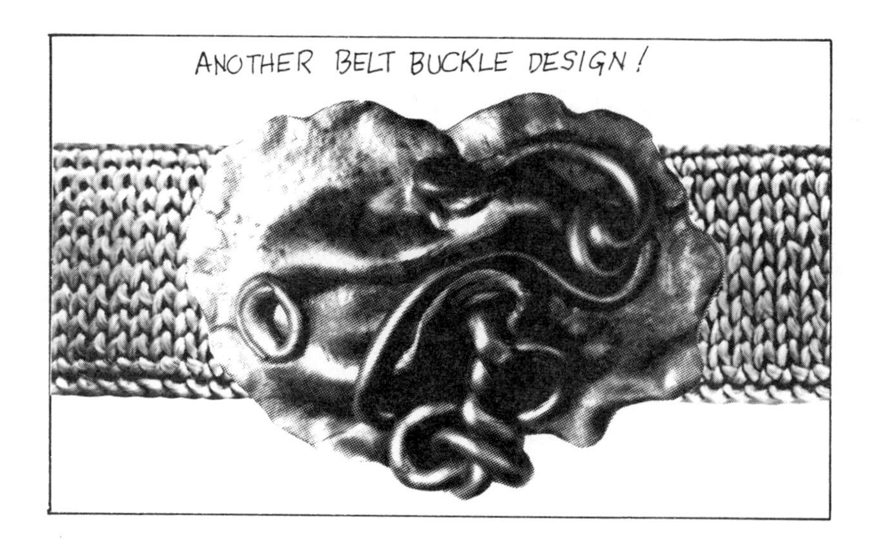

Buckle B4

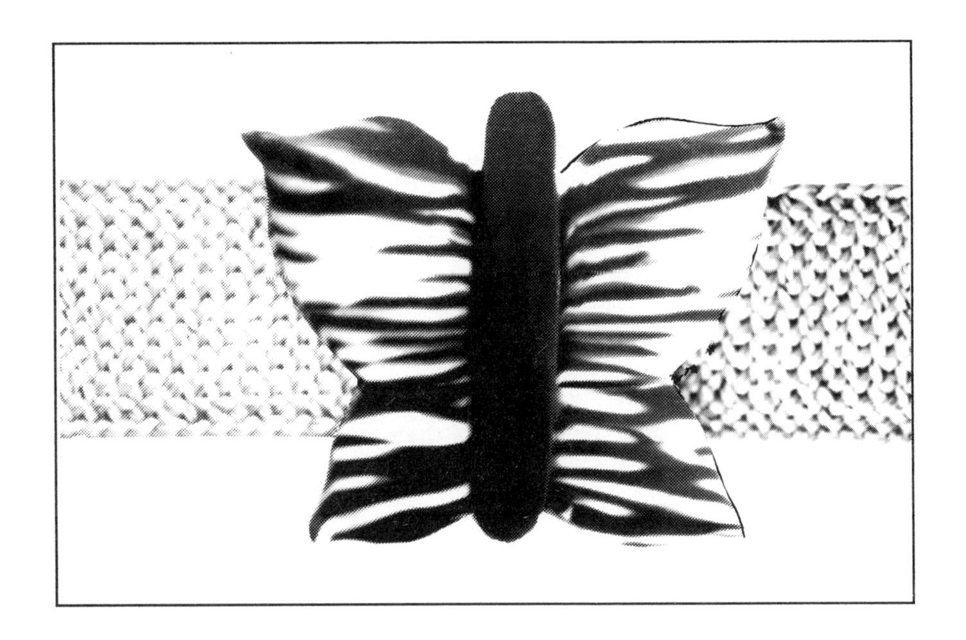

Butterflies are so much fun to make. You have so many colors and shapes to choose from. This one is made from black, green and yellow. It is used on a sand 2-inch stretch belt or a black one.

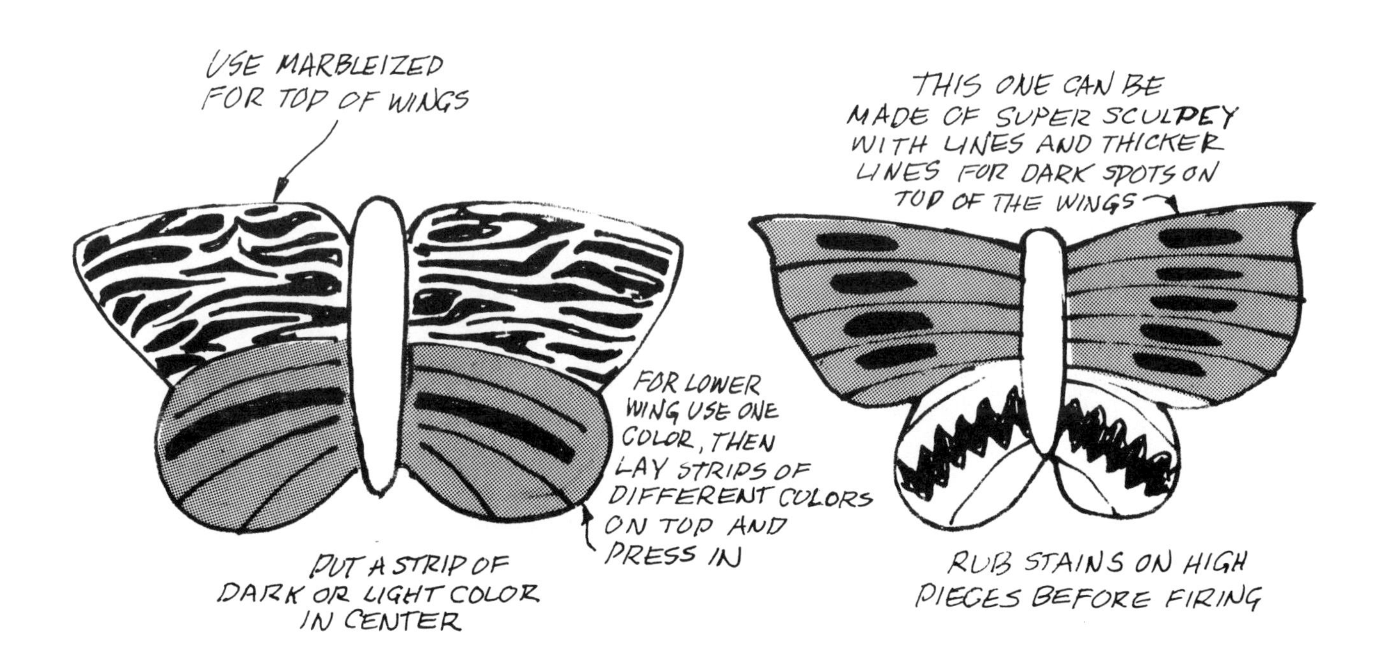

Buckle B4

Use four small rolls from a two-ounce piece of black. Soften, and roll into a long tube. Then do the same with three small rolls from a two-ounce piece of green and yellow. Twist them together into the typical candy cane and keep making it tighter so that you see the lined texture running around it. Then flatten it and roll out **(Fig. 47).**

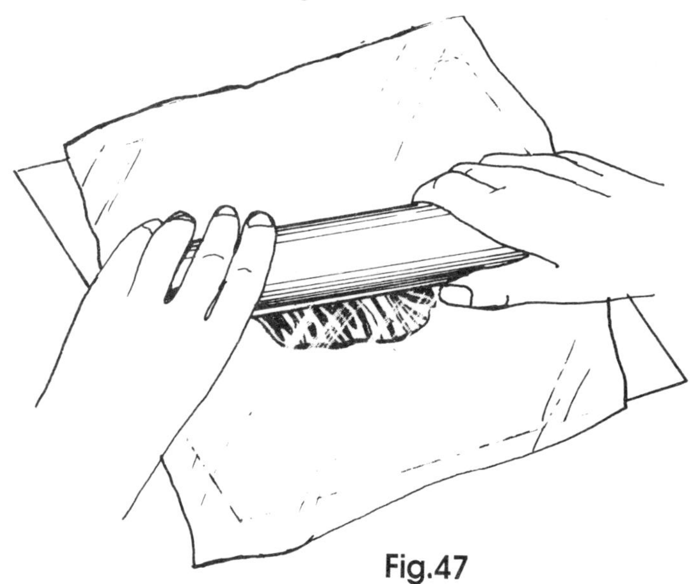

Fig.47

Cut out using pattern B4 Part 1. Soften, and roll out two small rolls of black and cut out using pattern Part 2. Fire, and glue on a belt buckle fastener. This piece is nice with no glaze, or you can glaze if you wish to.

Pinch the ends of the wings. **(Fig .48)**

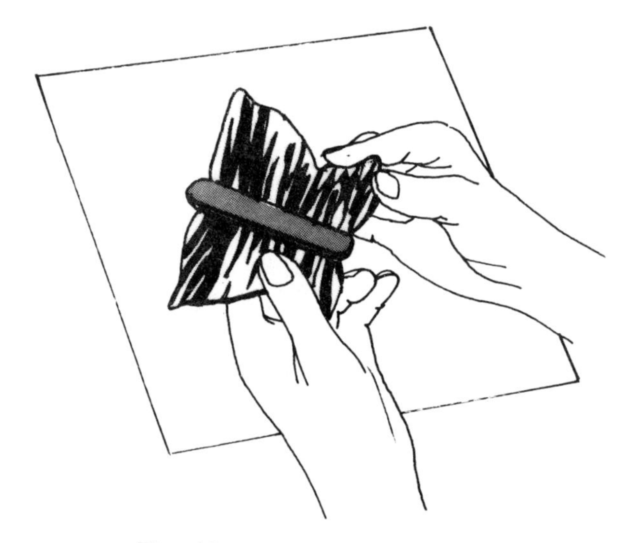

Fig.48

BUCKLE B5

This belt is very popular because you don't have to use any fasteners. It is simply a metallic bronze background and belt holder with an off-white flower with a black center. See special section on belting for directions for making a belt.

USE SUPER SCULPEY FOR THE END PIECES. RUB IN GOLD METALLIC EYE SHADOW.

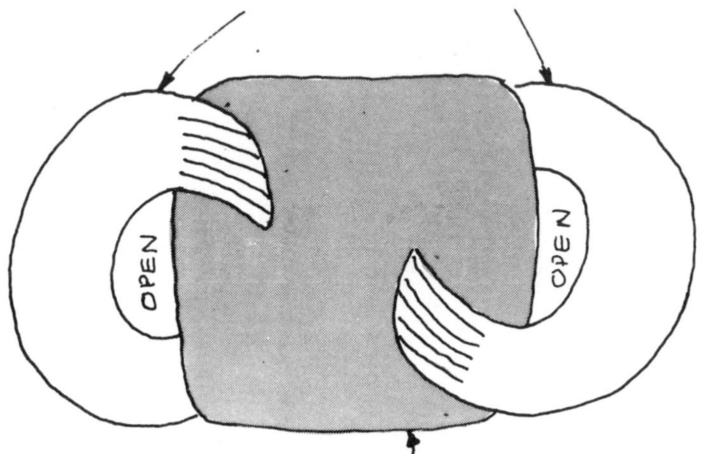

USE METALLIC BRONZE FOR THE TWO END PIECES AND LEAVE OPENINGS FOR THE BELT TO GO THROUGH.

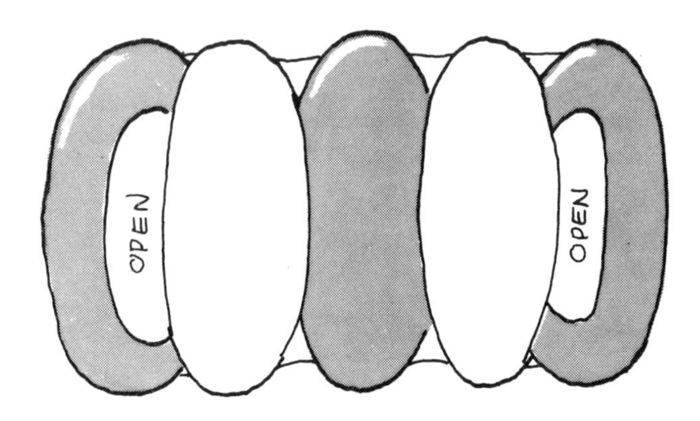

Buckle B5

Soften a two-ounce piece of metallic bronze and roll it out to a little more than 1/8 inch thick. Cut out, using pattern Part 1. Soften and roll to 1/8 inch thick – one half of a two-ounce package of pearl. Cut out using pattern Part 2, placing it on Part1.**(Fig.49).**

Press down to make it adhere. Put in deep lines where shown on pattern. Then take one small tube of 2-ounce black and roll it into a roll 1/8 inch thick and cut out, using pattern Part 3. Place this in center of flower and press to adhere.

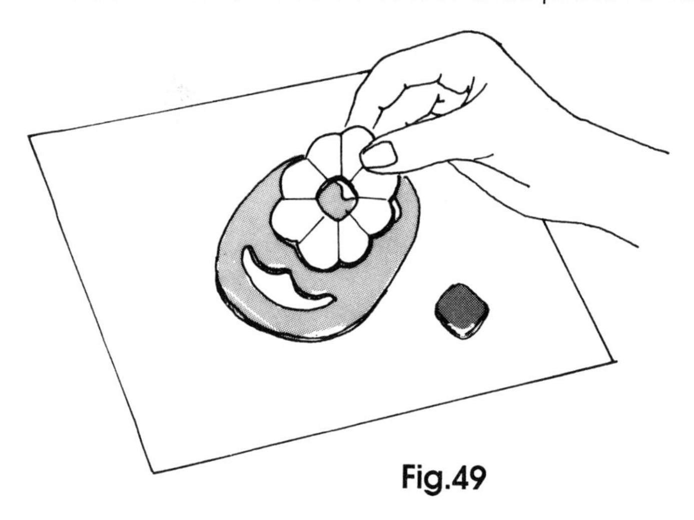

Fig.49

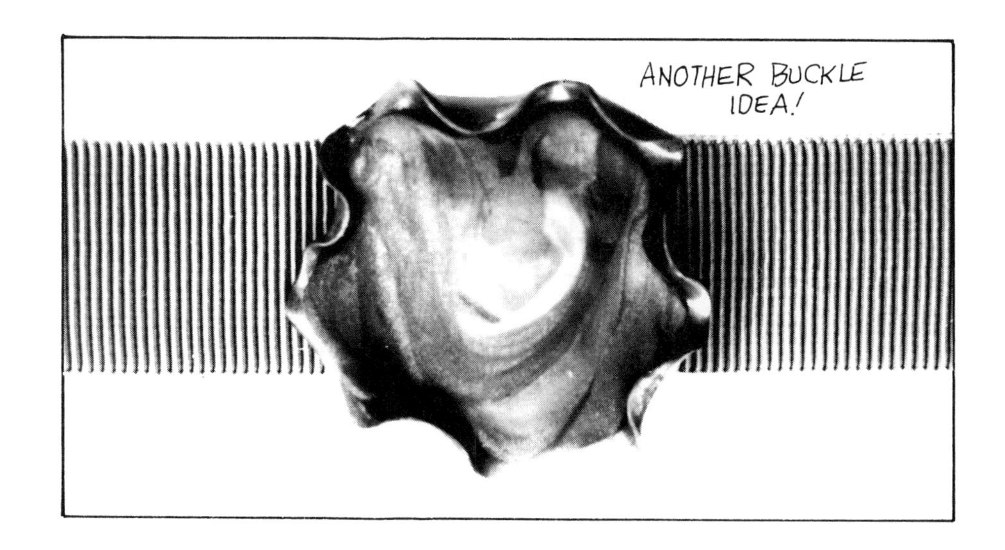

BUCKLE B6

This "flower garden" is a very happy, colorful belt buckle. Any number of colors can be used on it. Shades of greens with copper and gold glitter have been used for the stems. Blues, yellows, pinks and white are used for the flowers

---

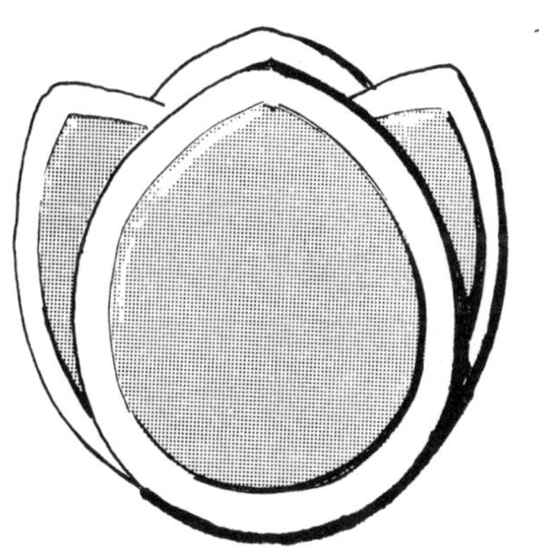

HOW ABOUT RED AND WHITE?
OR BLACK AND WHITE?

TULIPS COME IN ALL COLORS—TRY ALL COMBINATIONS!

Buckle B6, continued

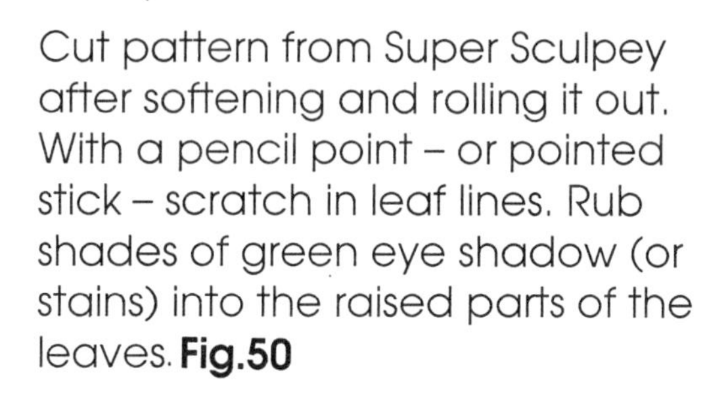
Cut pattern from Super Sculpey after softening and rolling it out. With a pencil point – or pointed stick – scratch in leaf lines. Rub shades of green eye shadow (or stains) into the raised parts of the leaves. **Fig.50**

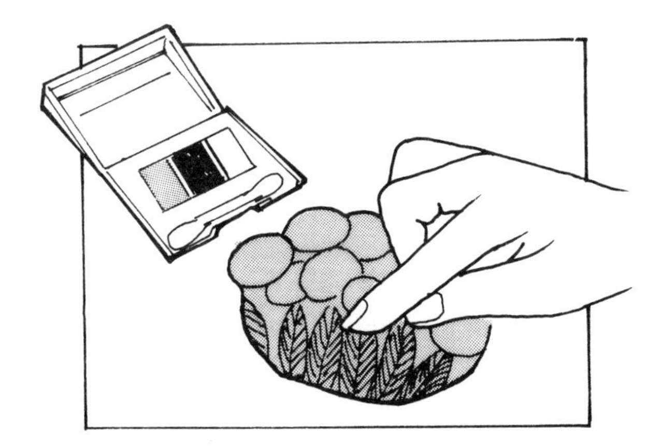

Fig.50

Form about 8 to 10 balls of different shades of colors for the flowers. Press them very thin, then place in the flower area – overlapping one another. Press them down. **Fig.51**

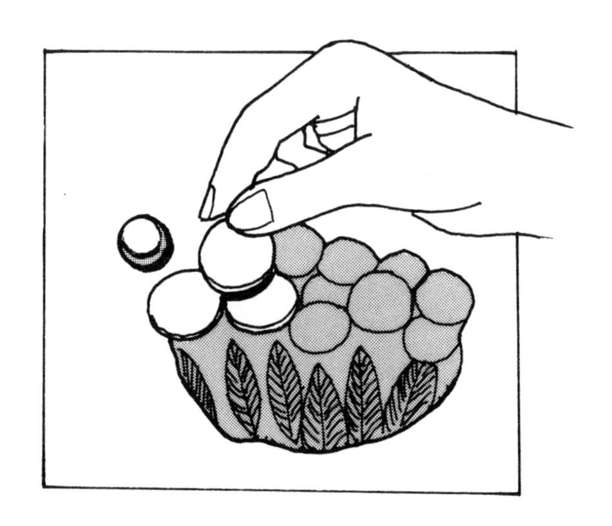

Fig.51

With a pencil point make centers in the flowers. **Fig.52.** Before firing, arch it a bit to fit your waist. Put a piece of compound under it to hold it up in the middle. Fire at 250° for 30 minutes or until lines in the leaves are dark. When it has cooled, if the flowers do not adhere, put a little epoxy under them. Glaze with a clear glaze or spray. Glue fasteners on the back with epoxy. Remember epoxy can also be used as a glaze if you care for a shiny look.

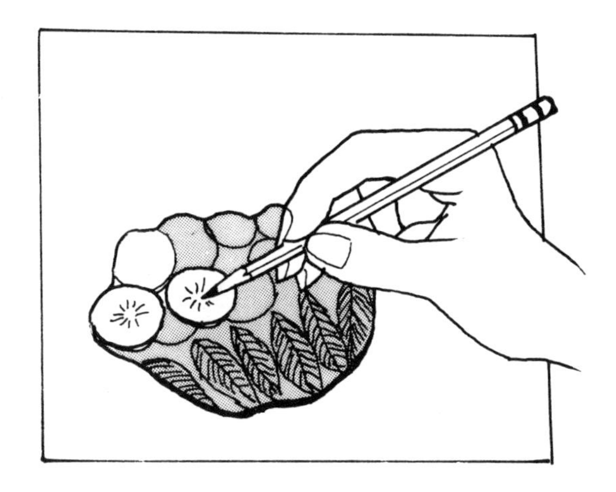

Fig.52

BUCKLE B7

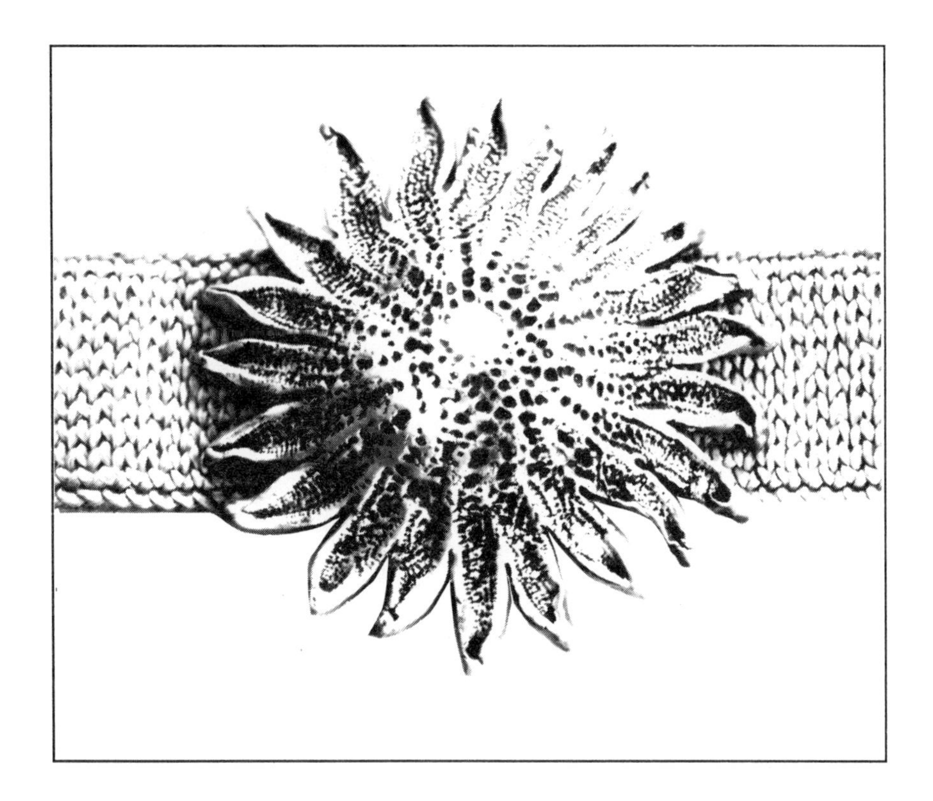

The pattern for this belt buckle is a dry starfish. It has a lot of texture on the top. That was the part that was pressed into the compound to achieve the design. Directions follow.

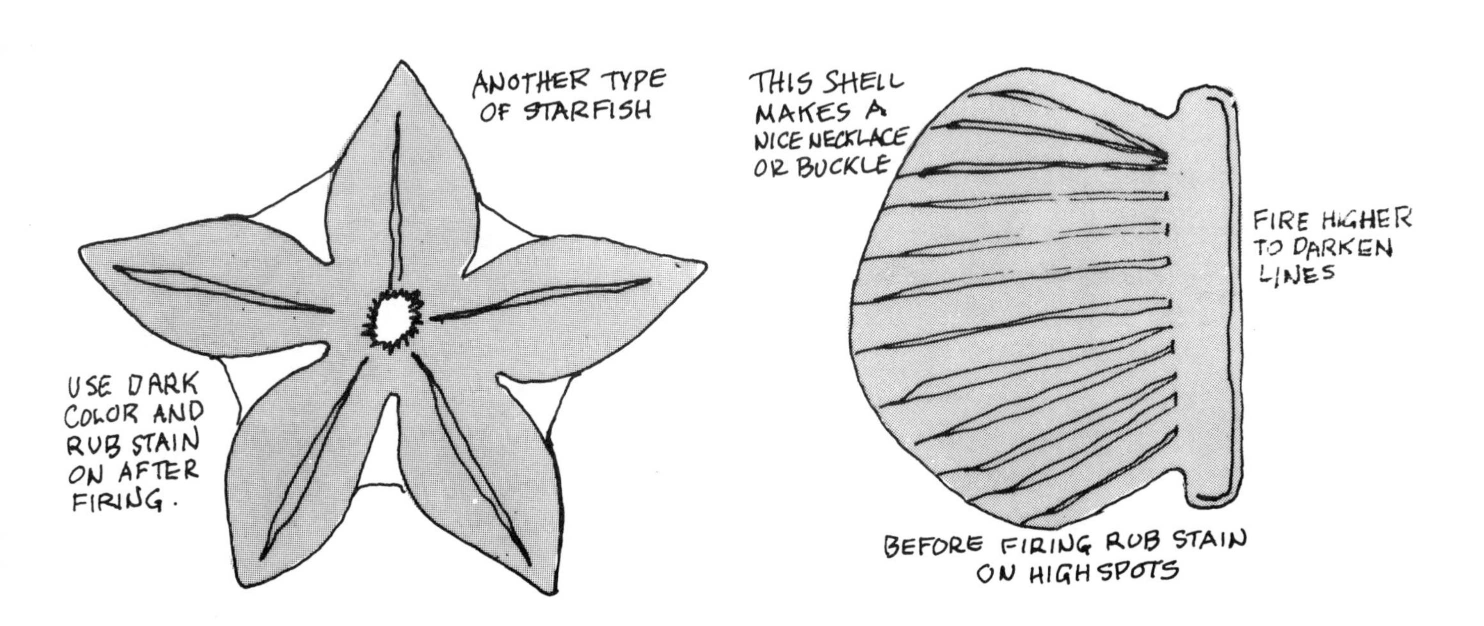

Buckle B7, continued

Get a starfish from a craft shop.

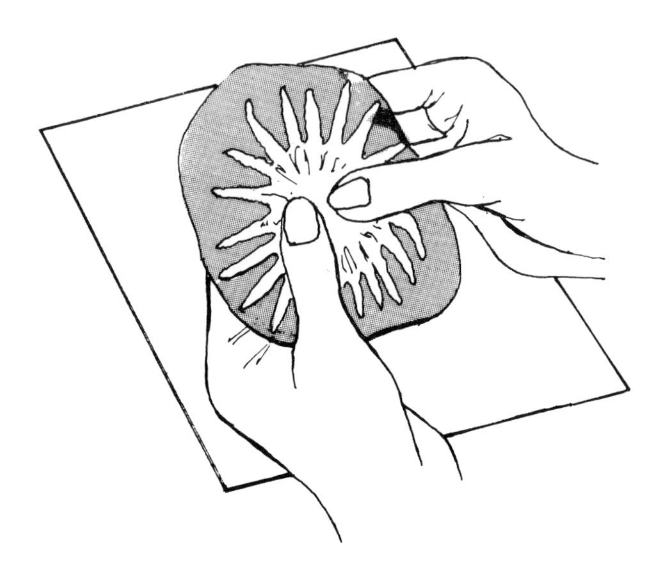

Roll out one 2-ounce package of brown. Press textured side of starfish on it and press in **(Fig. 53).**

Fig. 53

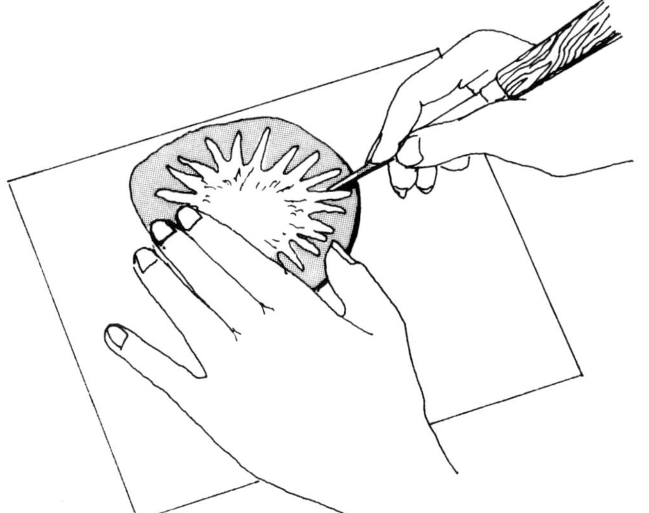

Then cut around it. **(Fig. 54)**

Fig. 54

Pick it up and press the ends together to make a soft point**(Fig.55).** Put a lump of compound under center (see General Instructions) so that it will fire with a raised center.

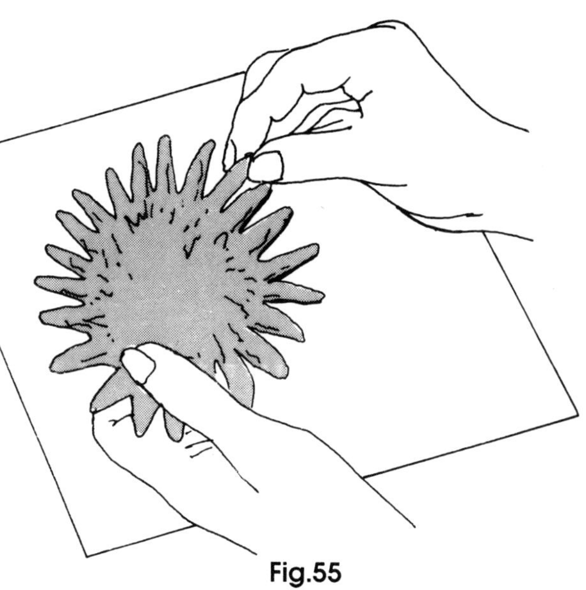

Fig.55

BUCKLE B8

This buckle is made by simply rolling out tubes of different colors and pressing them together. Then have fun pressing all types of threads, glitter, etc., into it.

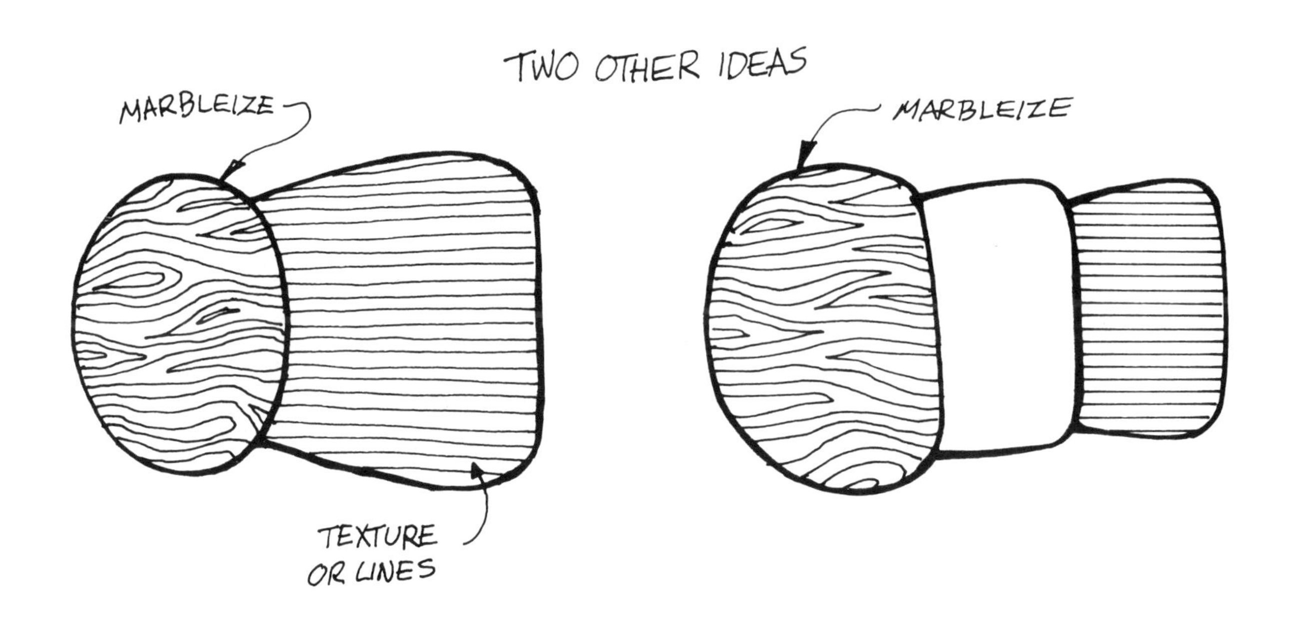

Buckle B8, continued

Roll 5 tubes of black and 2 tubes of beige (brown with white kneaded into it) and 2 tubes of white. Make each of them about 2" long and about 1/2" thick. Flatten them slightly. **Fig.56**

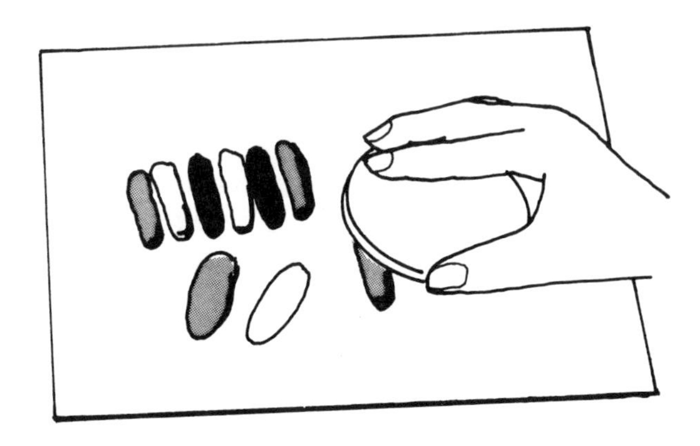

Fig.56

Fig.57

Lay them out – slightly overlapping one another. **Fig.57.** Alternate the colors. Lay them on paper.

Place paper over the piece, then roll slightly with a roller. Remove paper and sprinkle on gold glitter. Press in some threads and other trims you want to. Firing will not hurt these. Then roll again in both directions. Fire 20 minutes at 250º. Then spray on several coats of clear glaze . **Fig.58.** Put a piece of compound under the piece when firing to keep the curved contours of the waist.

Fig.58

BUCKLE B9

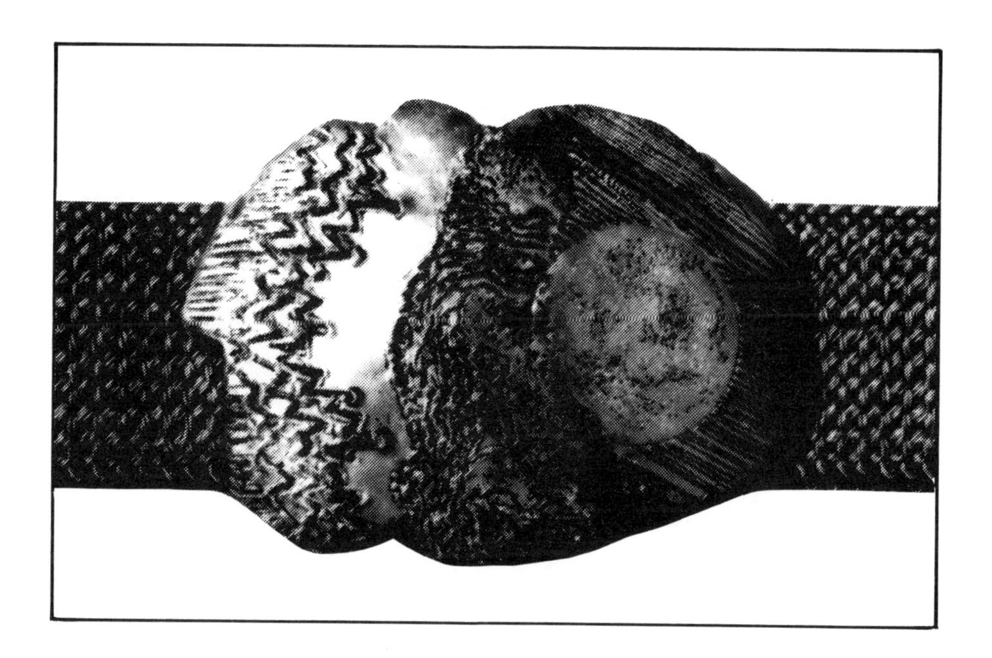

This buckle can be made in a variety of shapes. It is made from Super Sculpey and fired until the lines darken. This is a secret way of obtaining the look the artist wanted for some of her designs.

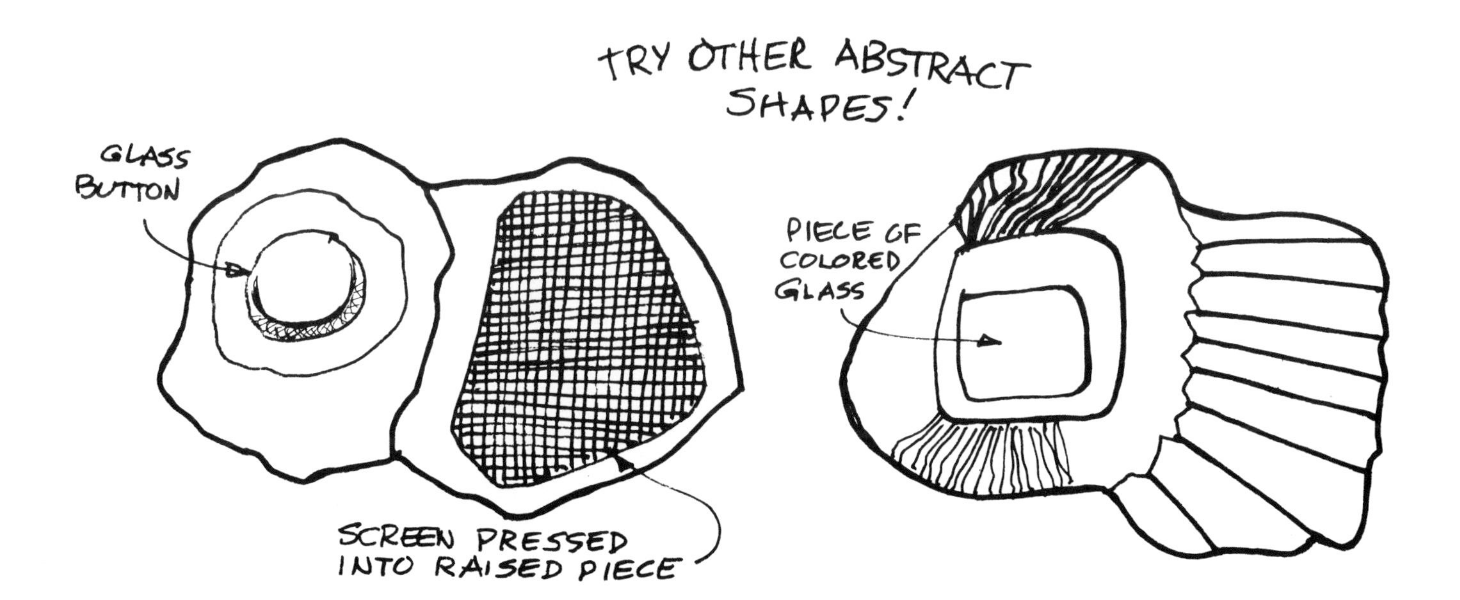

Buckle B9, continued

Cut pattern from Super Sculpey.
Draw in lines with sharpened pencil.
Also poke in the holes **(Fig.59)**

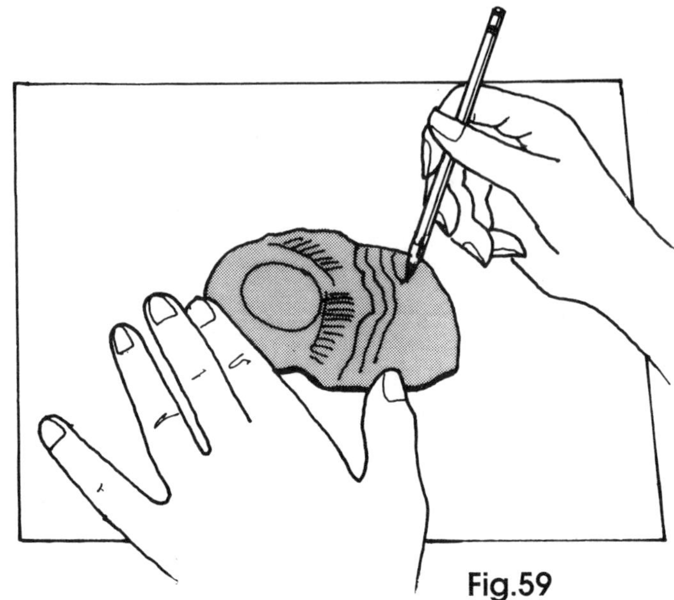

Fig.59

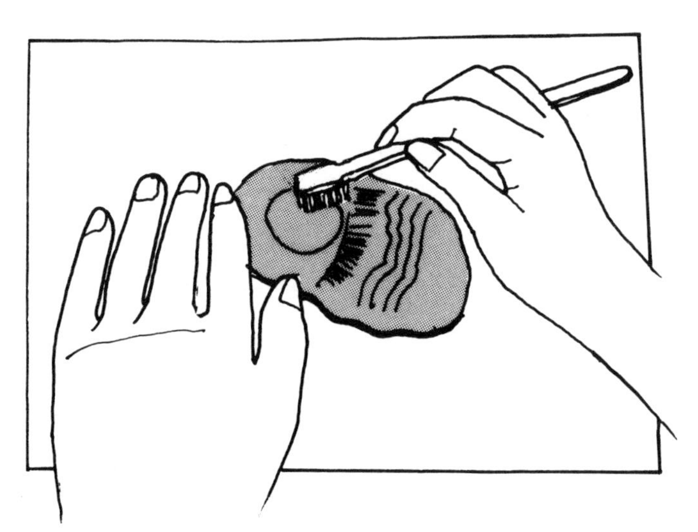

Fig.60

Using a tooth brush,
texture the circle part.
Fire 30 minutes at 250°
or until lines turn dark.
(Fig.60).

When cool, rub silver
on the high spots. Spray
clear glaze if you care to.
(Fig.61)

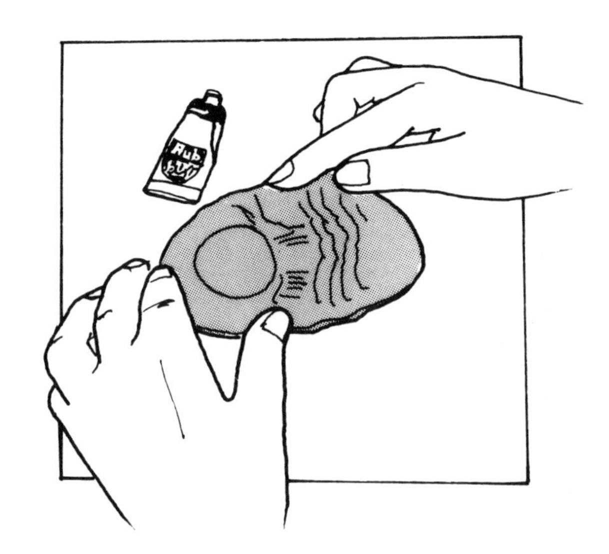

Fig.61

Necklaces
Beads

MAKING ROUND AND TUBULAR BEADS

Beads are such fun! You can make them all one color or multi-colored, round, square or tubular. Pieces left over from making a buckle or necklace – or anything else – can be made into a bead of some kind. I have a string of beads I call my "crazy string". It is all colors, shapes and sizes.

ROUND BEADS

When you make round beads simply pull a piece from the softened material the size you want the bead to be **(Fig. 5).** Roll it in the palm of your hand **(Fig. 6).**

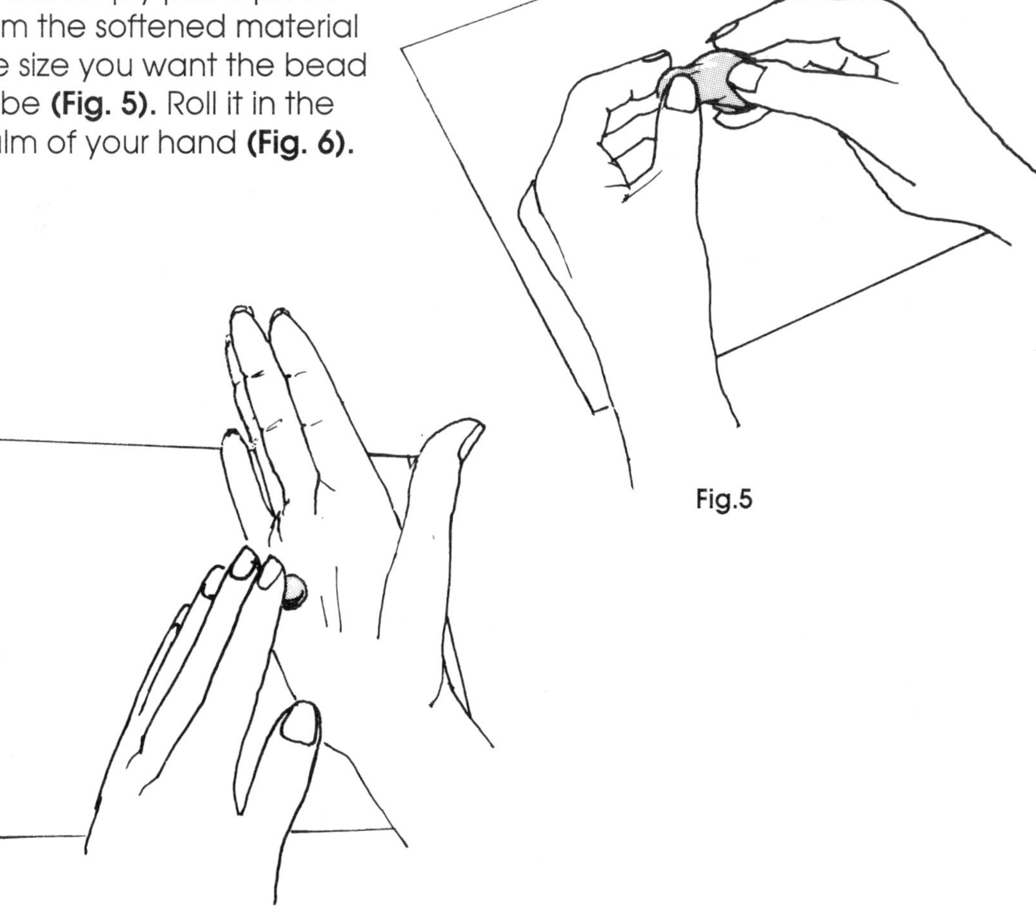

Fig.5

Fig.6

MAKING ROUND AND TUBULAR BEADS, Continued

Make the number and size of beads you are planning to use before putting holes in them. Put them on a tray (or anything flat) and place in your refrigerator for a couple of hours. This will make them a bit firmer when you put holes in them.

Use a pointed pencil or wire the diameter of a coat hanger to put holes in them. It is best to put a hole in one side, press the other side on a flat surface, then turn over and press excess material out. **(Fig. 7)**

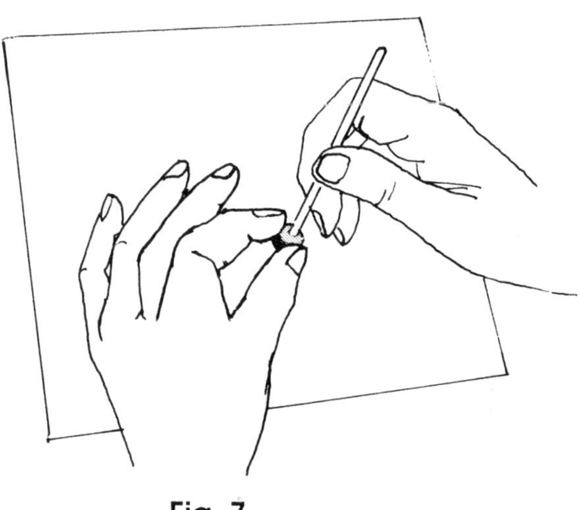

Fig. 7

TUBULAR BEADS

After softening, roll 1/2 of a two-ounce piece of material between the palm of your hands and then roll it on the wax paper. Starting in the middle roll gently, sliding your fingers out to the edges as you roll. Do this until your get the thickness you want, then with your knife cut the roll into the length of tubular beads needed. **(Fig. 8)**

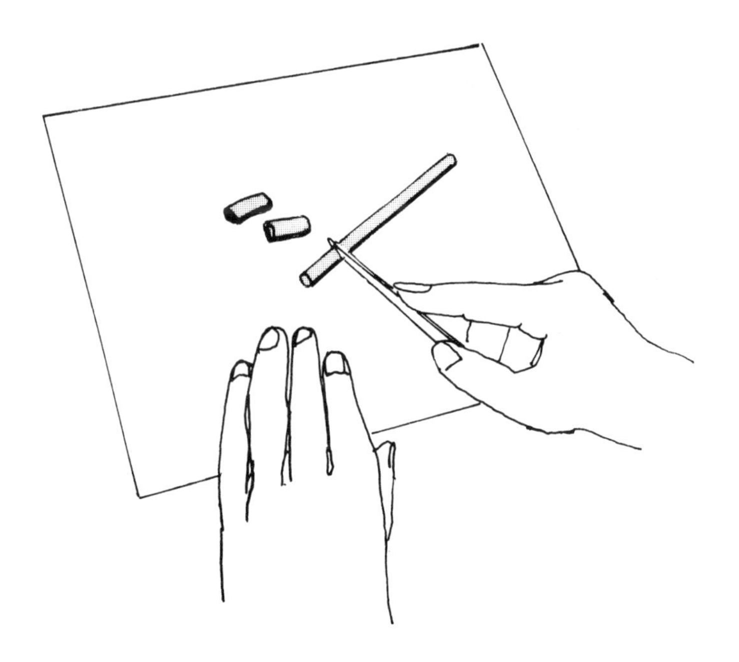

Fig.8

TUBULAR BEADS, continued

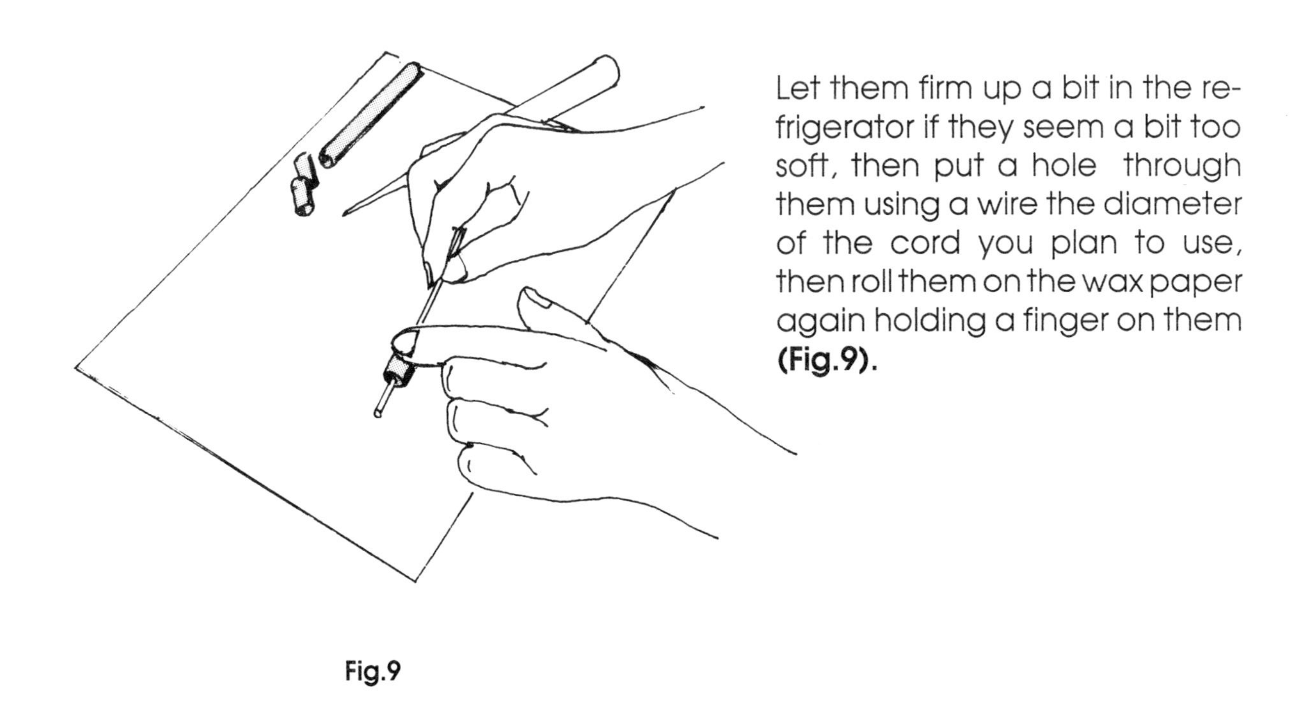

Let them firm up a bit in the refrigerator if they seem a bit too soft, then put a hole through them using a wire the diameter of the cord you plan to use, then roll them on the wax paper again holding a finger on them **(Fig.9).**

Fig.9

After you have made the beads, put them on a flat tin to bake (a cookie sheet is a natural for this). See the part on baking – or as I prefer to call it– "**Firing and Glazing**", page 18.

Stringing Beads and Necklaces

When making a string of beads you want to fasten with a clasp or hook fastener string them on tigertail wire or a bead cord (see **SOURCES**). With these cords you need to make only a small hole in your beads. You will need four crimp beads, a jump ring and an adjustable hook.

crimp bead   adjustable hook   jump ring

Measure the cord or wire you have chosen to use about 8" longer than the finished necklace is to be. Thread this through two crimp beads and the adjustable hook.

Then thread it back through the crimp beads pulling it firm so the adjustable hook is tightened against the crimp bead. Press the crimp beads together with pliers, then proceed to string your beads – being sure you put the loose end of the cord or wire through the first few beads. When you come to the end, string on two more crimp beads and jump ring. (You may use more than one jump ring if you want to make it adjustable).

String the cord or wire back through a few beads, pulling jump ring close to the crimp beads. Press these crimp beads together. You may use a barrel screw type clasp if you care to – instead of the jump ring and the adjustable hook.

barrel fastener

If you are making a pendant with no beads and want an attractive cord for it, cut 3 strands of soutache and thread them through a fastener on the back of the pendant. Tie a knot on each side of the fastener and then braid the cords on each side. Knot the end and cut close to the knot – then apply a drop of **Elmer's Glue** and blend it in to secure the knot.

If you want the braid cord with beads and a pendant just make the holes in the beads large. Test to see how large they need to be for three strands of cord to go through.

Stringing Beads and Necklaces, continued

A thick cord like N8 is made by wrapping soutache around a cord used for making pillows, etc. You may just use some thick drapery cord if you prefer. It comes in different colors in the drapery notions. When using a thick cord use two bullet ends with a loop. Use glue to attach cord inside bullet ends.

bullet end

Then put a jump ring on each bullet end and any type of fastener you prefer using. Your local bead shop will help you with this or you may refer to the **SOURCES** page in the back.

This is a good time to tell you what fun it is to vary the beads you make by using all types of ready made beads, nuts from hardware, brass discs or anything else that seems to blend with the beads. Remember you never have to make your necklace from all the same materials. It's fun to be creative! Try it!

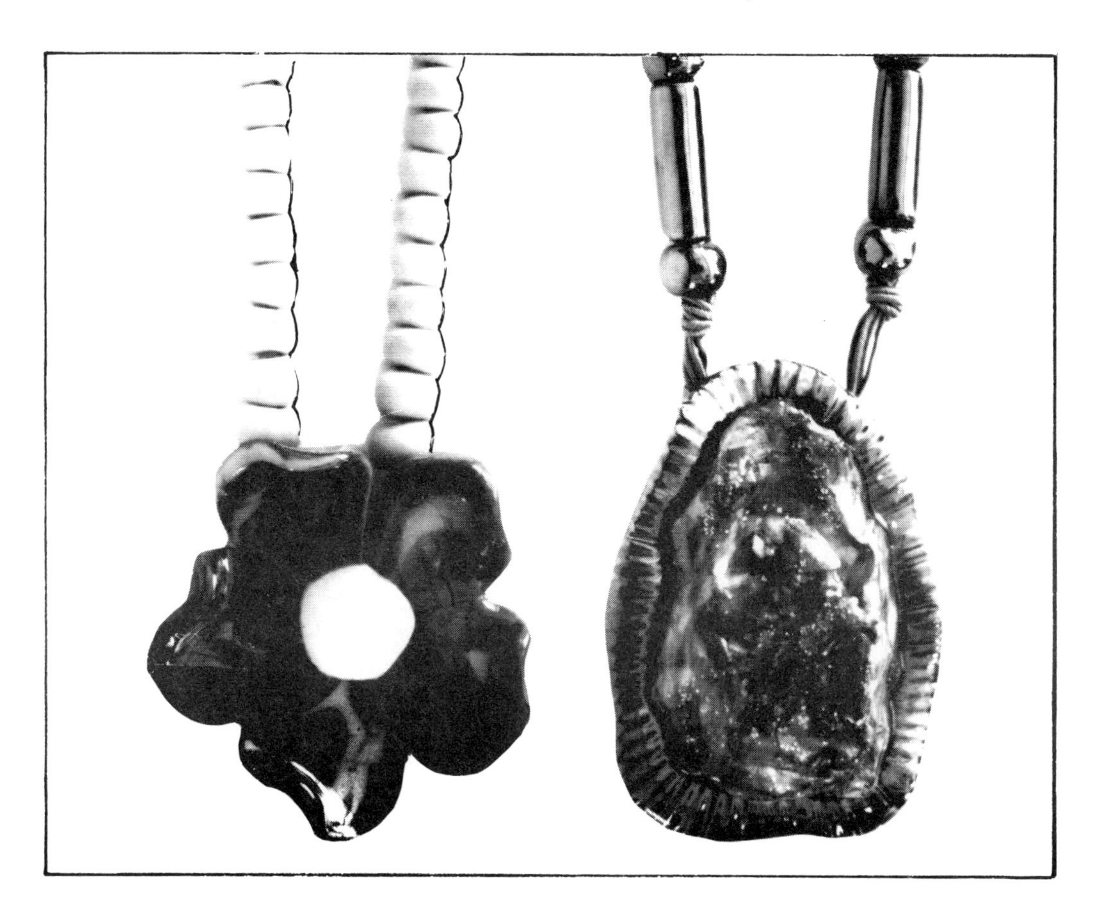

Necklace N1 Necklace N1A

Directions for making Necklace N1 begin on the next page. Necklace N1A is made in much the same way. Gold glass was used with a marbleized yellow and green tube around it. These are fired together to get a good fit. It does not hurt the glass to fire it. The glass may be purchased at most stained glass shops. After firing they are glued on white discs. Then it is assembled the same way N1 is.

Necklace N1

For this necklace use the following:

1 2-ounce Blue
2 rolls from a 2-ounce piece of white
2 rolls from a 2-ounce piece of red. **Fig.10**

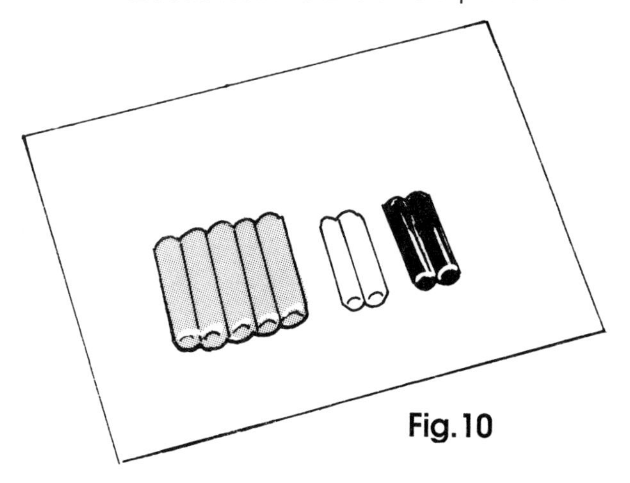

Fig.10

Blend these thoroughly together to get a violet shade. Add more white – or more black – depending on what shade you want.

After blending thoroughly, roll it out until you get about a 1/8" thickness. cut out one 3-inch circle and one 2-inch circle. Empty food cans are great for doing this – see **Fig.11**.

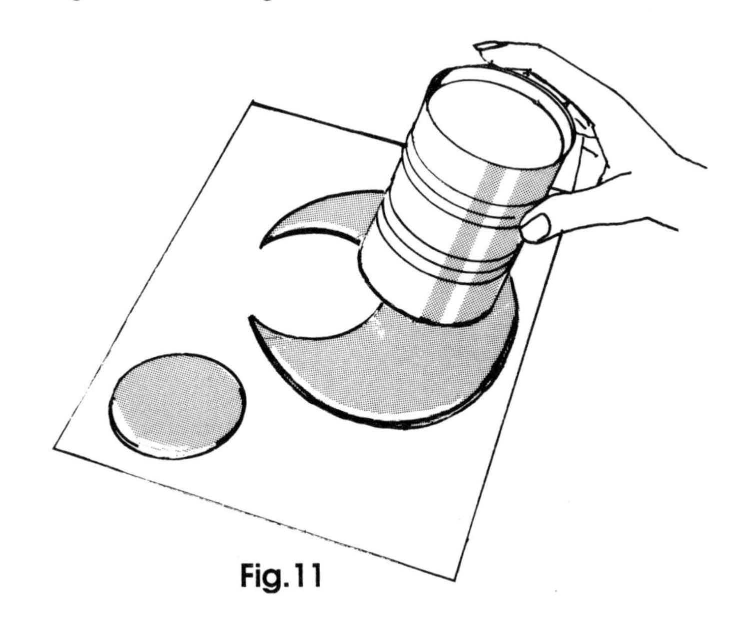

Fig.11

Necklace N1, continued

Roll the remaining violet into a tube. Roll one small roll from a 2-ounce piece of black and do the same with a small roll of green. Marbleize these by twisting (see **Marbleizing** on page 14).
Roll these out to about 1/8" and cut two circles from it – one 2-inch and one 1 1/2 inch. Place these on the two plain circles and put a hole in top and bottom of large circle (Use a wire the diameter of a coat hanger wire). Make the top hole larger so a double cord can be pushed through.
Put one hole in the small circle **(Fig.12).**

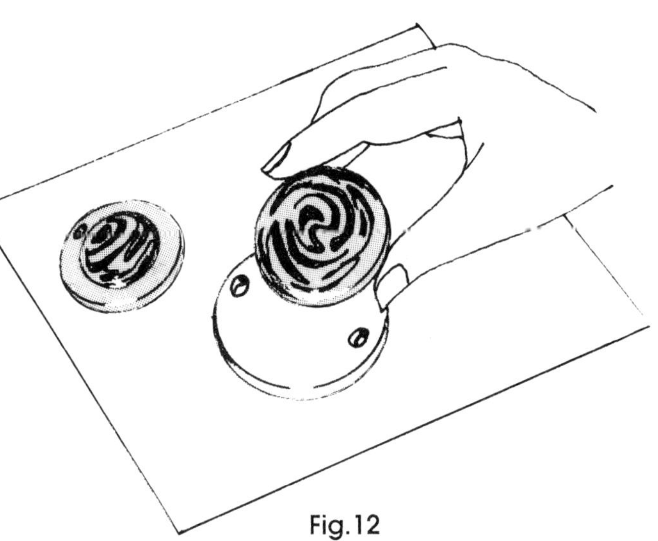

Fig.12

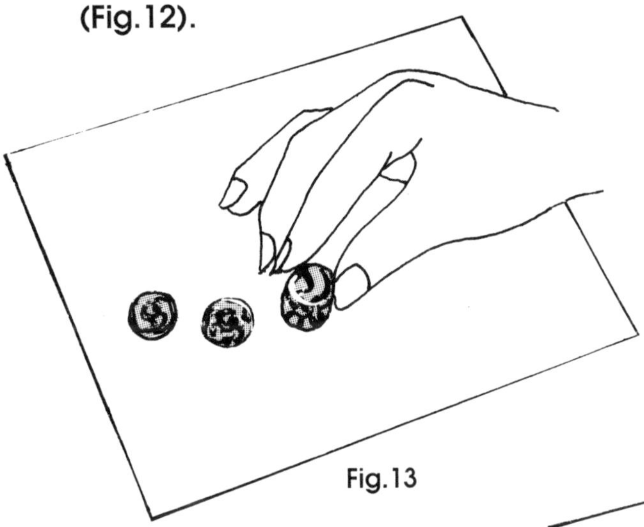

With remaining marbelized piece make a tubular bead and two round ones **(Fig.13).** Make holes in these large enough for double cord to go through.

Fig.13

After firing, assemble as shown **(Fig.14).**

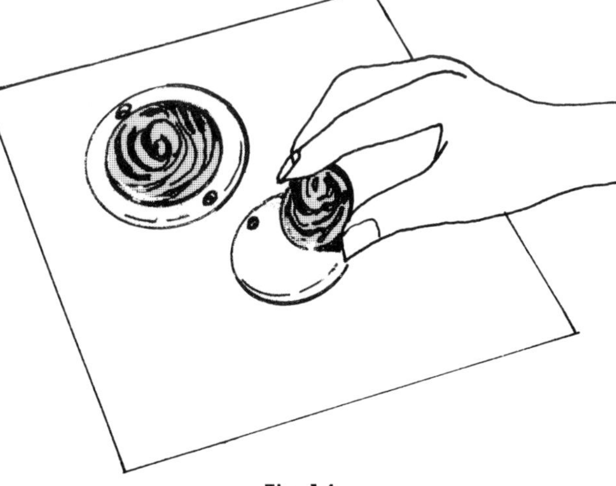

Fig.14

Necklace N1, continued

Glue marbled pieces on plain pieces. Use a ring (see No. F5) to fasten small one to the bottom of the large one. Glaze both circles if you want to. See page 18 on **Glazing**. Then select the cord and string through top of large circle **(Fig.15)** and string on a round bead, a tube and then another bead. Either knot the ends or make a long flat bead with the hole not going all the way through and glue on each end.

If you have a small marbleized piece left, roll it out and cut two small circles from it for earrings. Don't be afraid to make too much of a marbleized piece because left over pieces can be used for bolos, magnets or buttons.

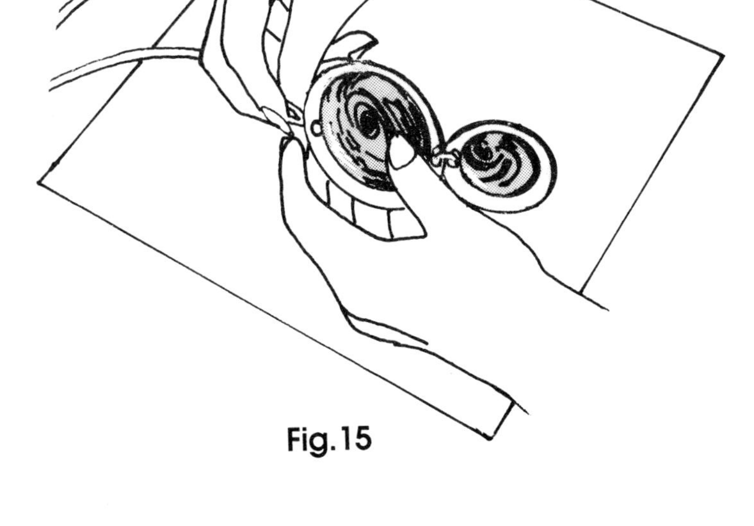

Fig.15

Necklace N2 | Necklace N2A

These two necklaces are made the same way. Directions for N2 follow. Necklace N2A is made with marbleized red, black and a small amount of white. Instead of beads, five strands of black cord are put through the loop to hold the flower pendant. The bullet end fasteners, jump rings, hook and cord may be purchased from sources listed in the back if you do not have a bead store in your area.

Necklace N2

Marbleize four small rolls of pink from a two-ounce piece with six rolls of purple. Roll out between wax paper to 1/8 inch thick. Using pattern on page 101, cut six petals. **Fig.16 .** Press it thinner, using a plaster disc or a block of wood.

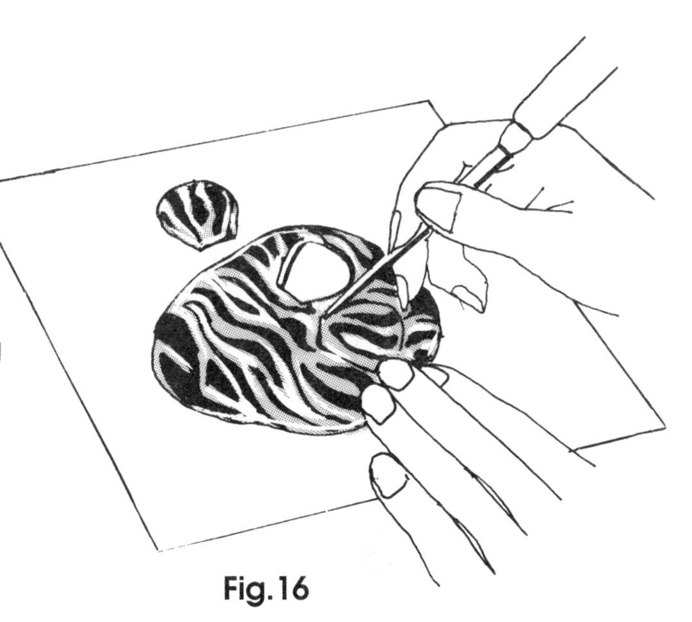

Fig.16

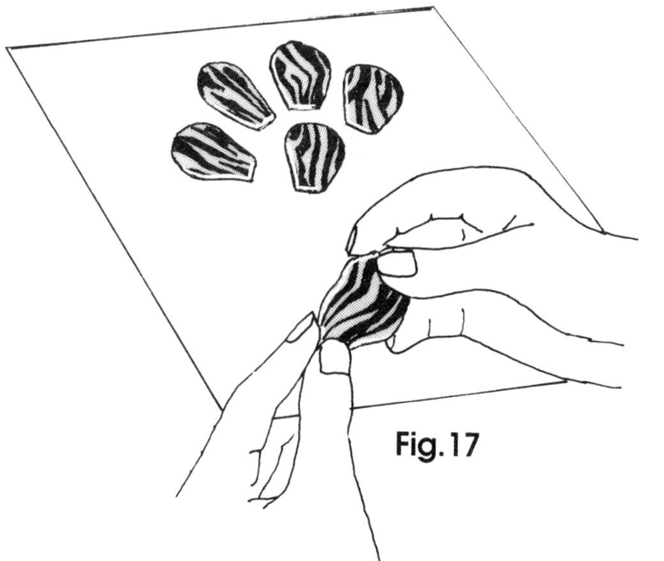

Fig.17

Pull to stretch it a bit longer. **Fig.17.** Round in the middle and pinch narrow end together. Place in a circle, **Fig.18 ,** overlapping them.

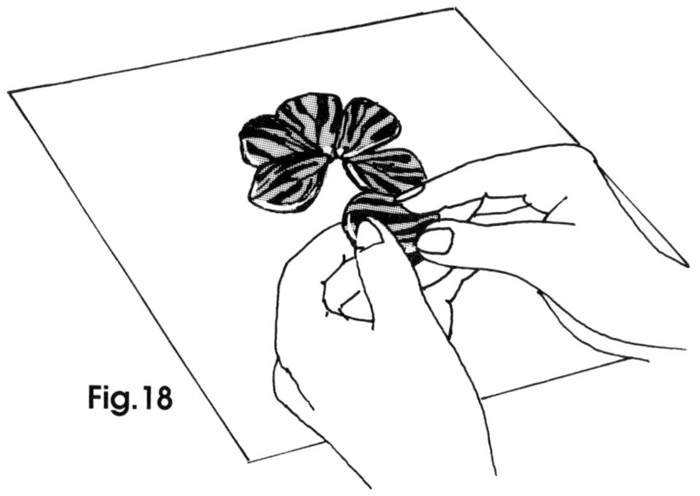

Fig.18

Necklace N2, continued

Press flat in center, using handle of knife or stick. This provides a surface on which to glue the center piece. **(Fig.19)**

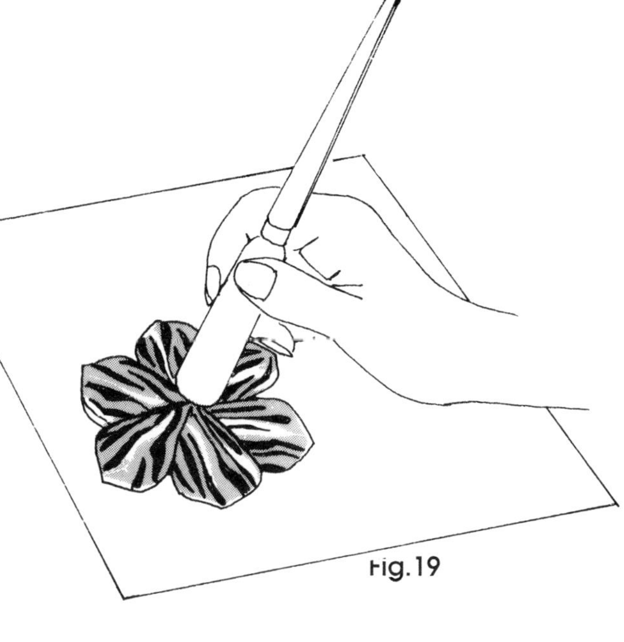

Fig.19

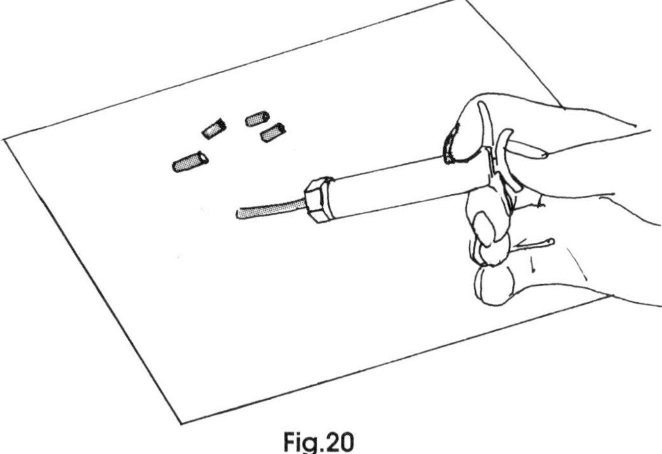

Fig.20

To make the center piece put a little softened pink in the extruder (see page 10) using the medium hole die. Extrude and cut them into 1/4 inch pieces **(Fig.20).**

Roll one end thinner and fit them together **(Fig.21)** Cut flat on the bottom and ***after*** the petal part has been fired fit the center piece into it. Carefully remove and fire. Glue in the center piece when both have been fired.

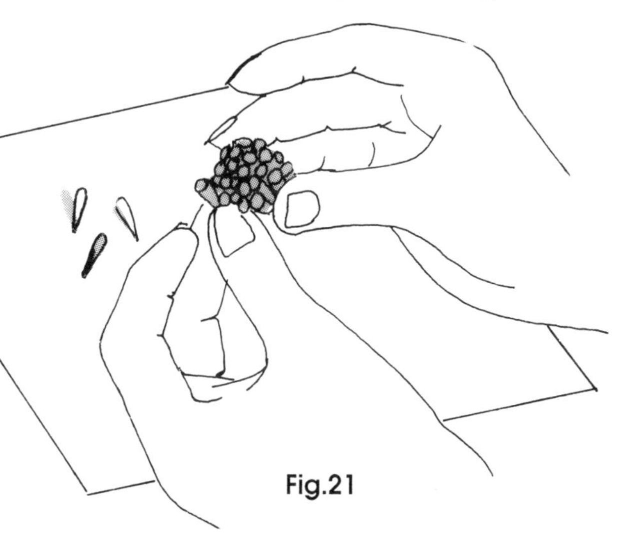

Fig.21

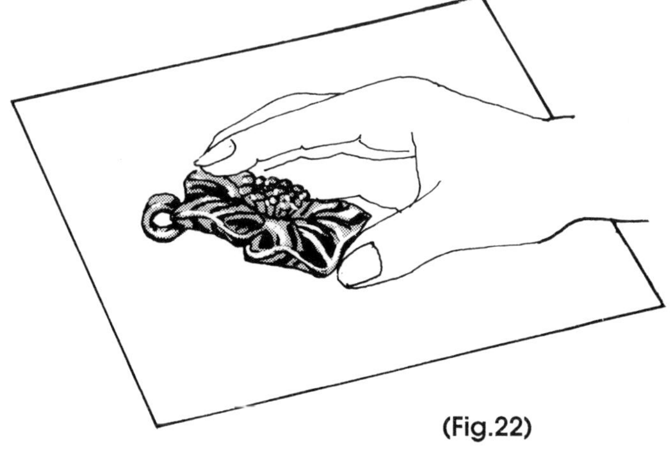

(Fig.22)

Cut a 2 inch long by 1/4 inch wide piece to glue on the flower back to hold the cord. Fold it into a loop and press flower on it at the top, letting loop extend above it **(Fig.22).**

Necklace N2, Continued

Make 36 beads from the pink compound. Put holes in them using wire. See **Beads** page 45. Make two thin tubes with the hole not going all the way through to glue on each end of cord. Be sure cord is long enough to tie it where you want to.

MORE PIN
DESIGNS!

Necklace N3

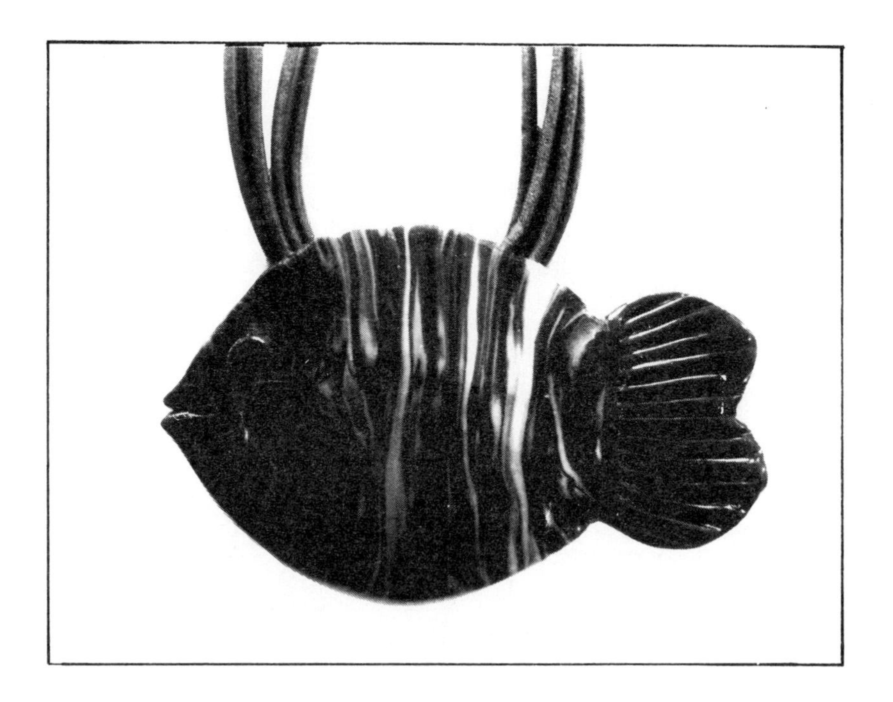

This fish necklace is made from marbleized orange, purple and red. The tail is purple and the eye is black. Five strands of dark blue cord are strung through the loop on the back. It is fastened with bullet end fasteners, jump rings and a hook. These may be found at your bead store or send for a catalog from the sources listed on the Source page at the back of the book. This fish may be made in a lot of different shapes and sizes.

Necklace N3

Take six rolls from a 2-ounce piece of purple compound and soften. Then roll it into a thick tube. Do the same with two rolls of orange and two rolls of red. Put them side by side and twist it so it is thicker in the middle **(Fig.23).**

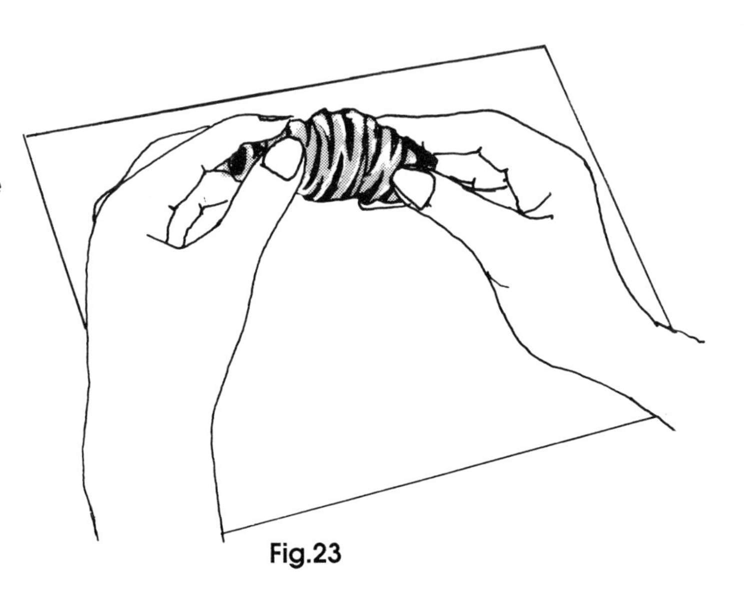

Fig.23

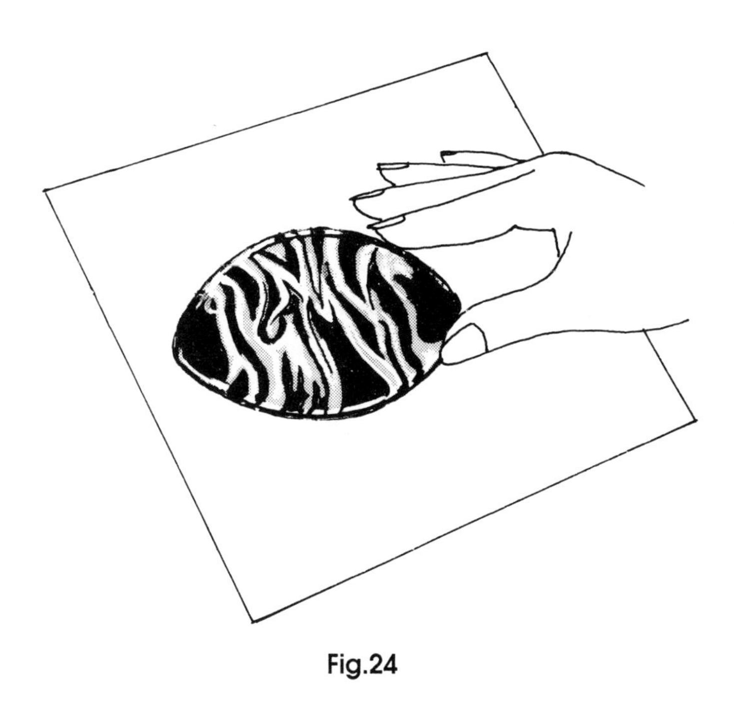

Fig.24

Flatten them out, then roll it out so that the stripes are vertical **(Fig.24).** When it looks similar to that shown in Fig. 24 you may use it as is and taper the end for a head and add plain purple for the tail as shown. Or you may use the pattern (page 103) to cut out the fish shape.

To make solid color tail and head, roll out two rolls of purple 1/8" thick. Use the pattern to cut them out and press in place on the fish. For the eye, press in a tiny piece of black. Cut a slit for the mouth. Then put a loop on the back for the cord to go through.(see Fig.30, page 65, for necklace loop). This one features five strands of blue waxed cotton (see **Source** section).

Necklace N4   Necklace N4A

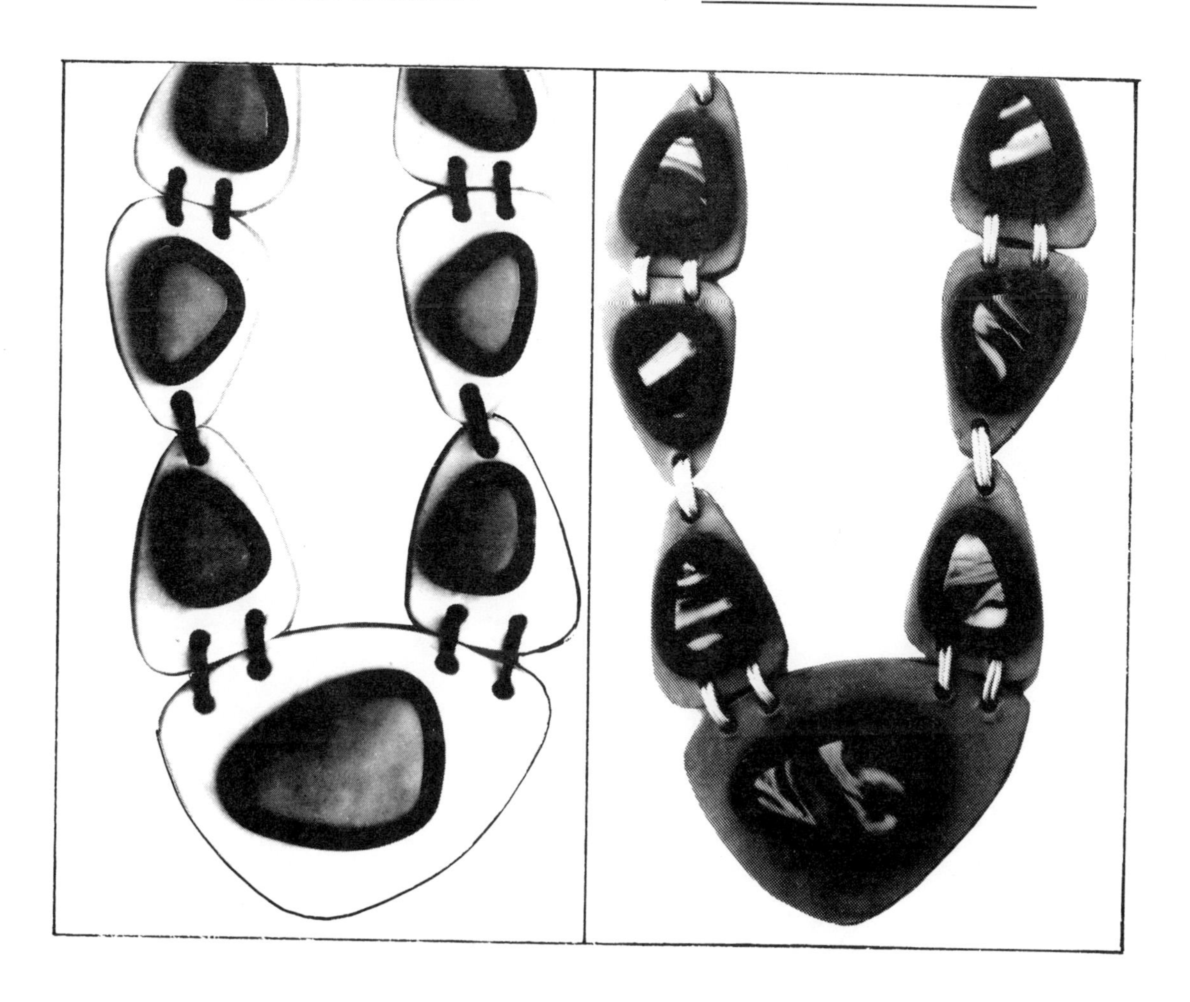

These are two very interesting pieces. They take a little more time to make but are well worth it. Directions for N4 are on the following page. N4A is made exactly the same. Metallic brass is used for the background. Metallic copper, green, black and metallic pewter are marbleized for the center pieces. Metallic copper is used to make the tubes around the marbleized pieces. String and finish them the same way you did N4.

Necklace N4

Use 1 1/2 ounces metallic bronze. Soften it and roll it out to about 1/8 inch thick. Cut bottom pieces of the necklace – 10 medium and one large, also two medium for earrings. Use patterns in pattern section page 103. Smooth edges and lay out. **Fig. 25.**

Then **marbleize** (see page 14):

2 rolls brown
1 roll chartreuse
1 roll metallic pewter
1 roll metallic copper
1 roll black

Fig. 25

Roll a little thicker than 1/8 inch and , using the pattern, cut out center pieces for necklace and earrings.

Soften four rolls from a two-ounce piece of metallic copper. Put a little at a time into the extruder with a 1/4 inch die. To make it easier to extrude: with your little finger put a little oil (any kind) into the channel. If you prefer you may roll by hand. Then fit a piece around the outside of the marbleized pieces. **Fig. 26.** Remove and smooth the cut edges together using the wooden tool. Make it round by putting finger inside and rolling it back and forth (**Fig. 27, next page).**

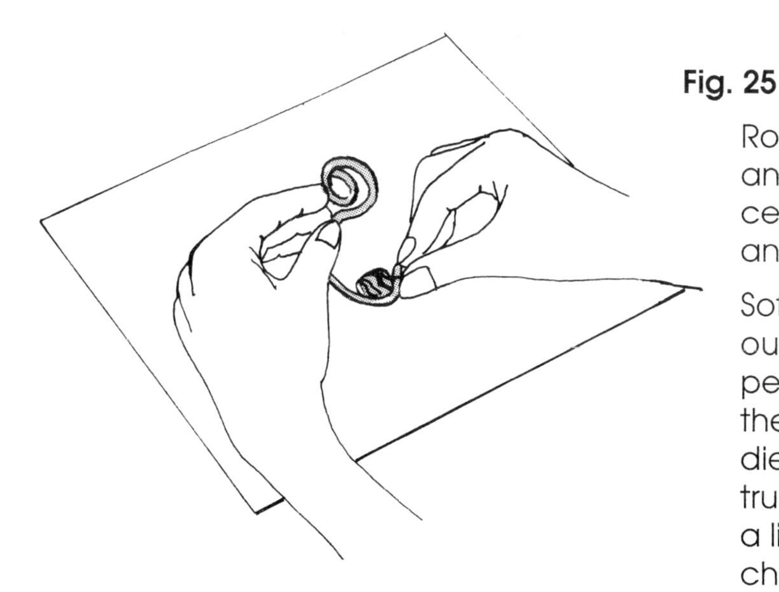

Fig. 26.

Necklace N4, continued

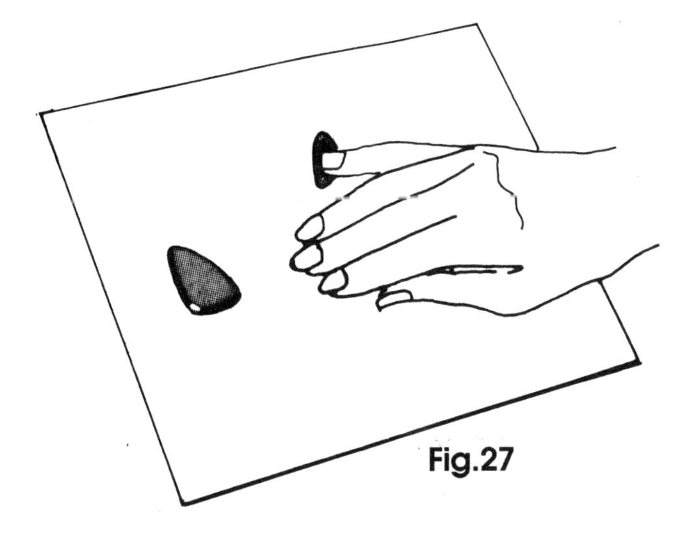

Fig.27

Place over top marbleized piece and gently push into place. Be sure that it fits close around the sides. **Fig.28** Do the same for all marbleized pieces

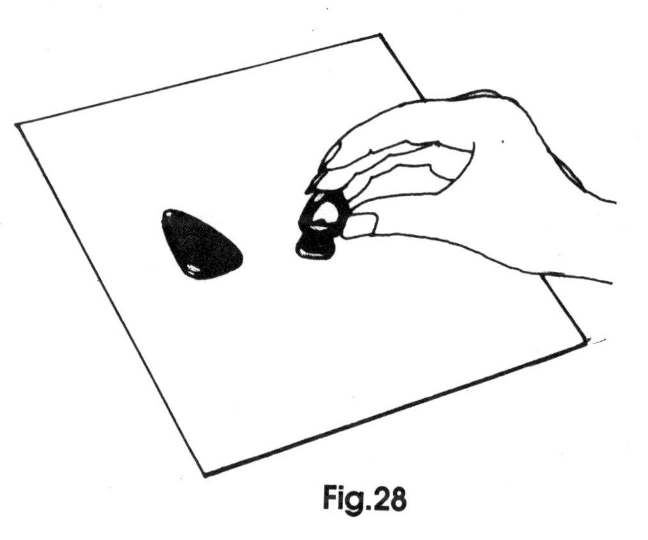

Fig.28

Put them all in place as shown in picture. Press them together. Follow marks in pattern and put in the holes. After firing, string cord through as in picture. Use clamping fastener, jump rings and adjustable necklace hook to fasten. See **FASTENERS** page 82 Get these at your bead or craft shop or from sources listed on the **SOURCES** page.

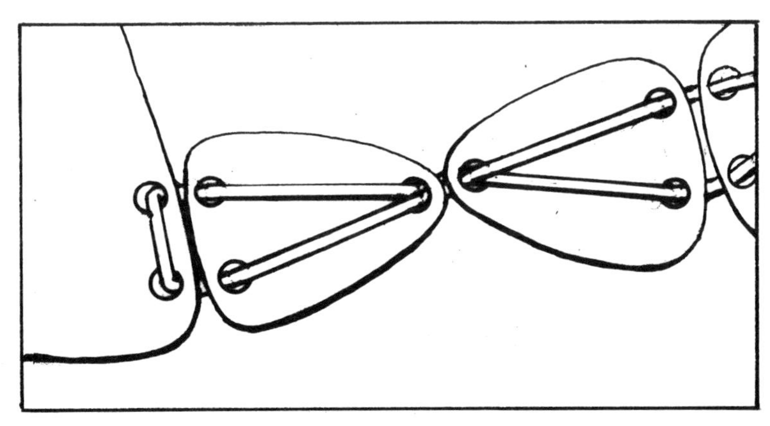

Detail showing backs of pieces with holes and stringing pattern.

Necklace N5

Necklace N5A

Two favorite beads with flower pendants. Directions for N5 start on the next page. The pendant for N5A is made from blue with yellow petals and a green center for the flower. The beads are made from marbleized blue and green. The tube is from the same marbleized piece. Use either a long cord for tying or use clamping fastener, jump rings and hook to fasten.

Necklace N5

Make 28 blue beads about 1/2 inch round and 30 white beads about 1/4 inch round. See section on bead making. Soften and roll out– about 1/8 inch thick – a piece of white. Cut out a circle and six pieces for petals using patterns from the pattern section. Smooth the edges..

Using a butter paddle (or any grooved piece) press each petal on it to create the lines. **Fig.29.**

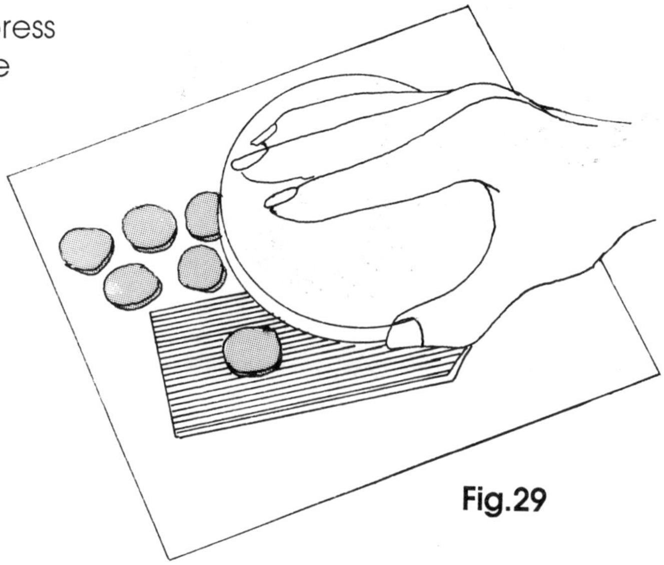

Fig.29

Gently round the center of each piece, overlapping as in picture of necklace. Press down in the center using end of the knife. Use about two rolls from a two-ounce piece of red. Soften and press through the extruder, using a 1/4 inch die. Cut into 1/2 inch pieces and make the center as you did for the center of Necklace N2. Then make a small loop on back for cord. Fire and string as in picture.

Necklace N6

Necklace N6A

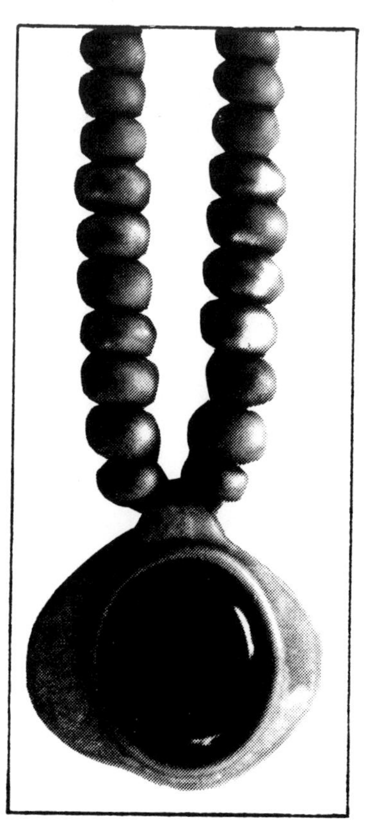

These two necklaces are made from metallic pewter. After following the directions on the next page for N6 you may want to make N6A also. Cut a shape similar to N6 and fit a glass nugget in it and put a tube around it. Use the metallic pewter or any color you care to for this necklace. The glass in this one is turquoise. Make the cord long enough for tying in the back.

Necklace N6

Soften one 2-ounce metallic bronze. Roll out to 1/8 inch thick and cut out 3 of pattern No. 6. Smooth the edges and pinch together slightly at the top, then roll a long piece back around the pencil and fasten. **Fig.30**

Make 14 round flat beads from metallic pewter, then from metallic bronze make 18 small ones. Or you may purchase 18 small brass beads. Fire and glaze if you care to, then string them as in picture.

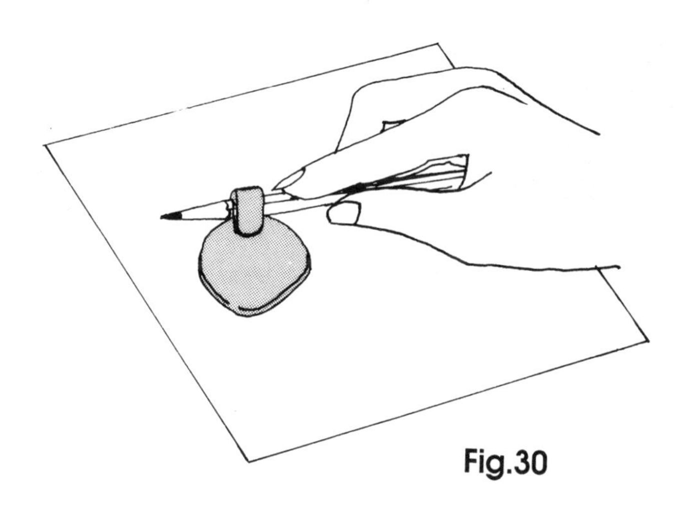

Fig.30

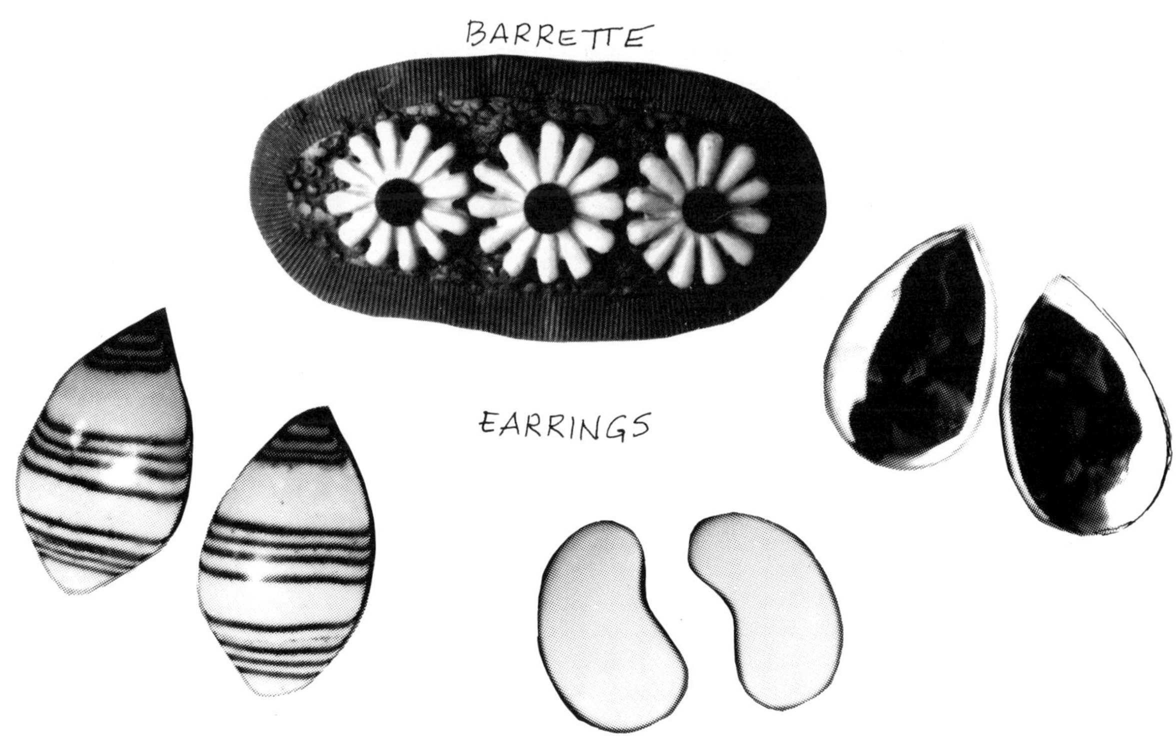

Necklace N7

This is another example of firing Super Sculpey a bit longer than usual. For this one Super Sculpey is softened and rolled about 1/8" thick. Use the pattern or cut your own abstract design. Place a cedar branch (as in photo) on it and press in hard. While it is still in place rub different colors of stain, watercolor inks or shades of eyeshadow on all the raised areas. Eyeshadows were used on the sample. Roll the top over with a pencil to form a loop to hold the cord. See photo.

When you have the color effect you like remove the branch. Fire at 250° for about 30 minutes or until lines from the cedar branch turn brown. The more metallic or pearlized powder you rub into it the more interesting the effect will be. Be sure to have ventilation in the room when firing. Open a window or door. After cooling, spray with a satin sealer.

Necklace N8

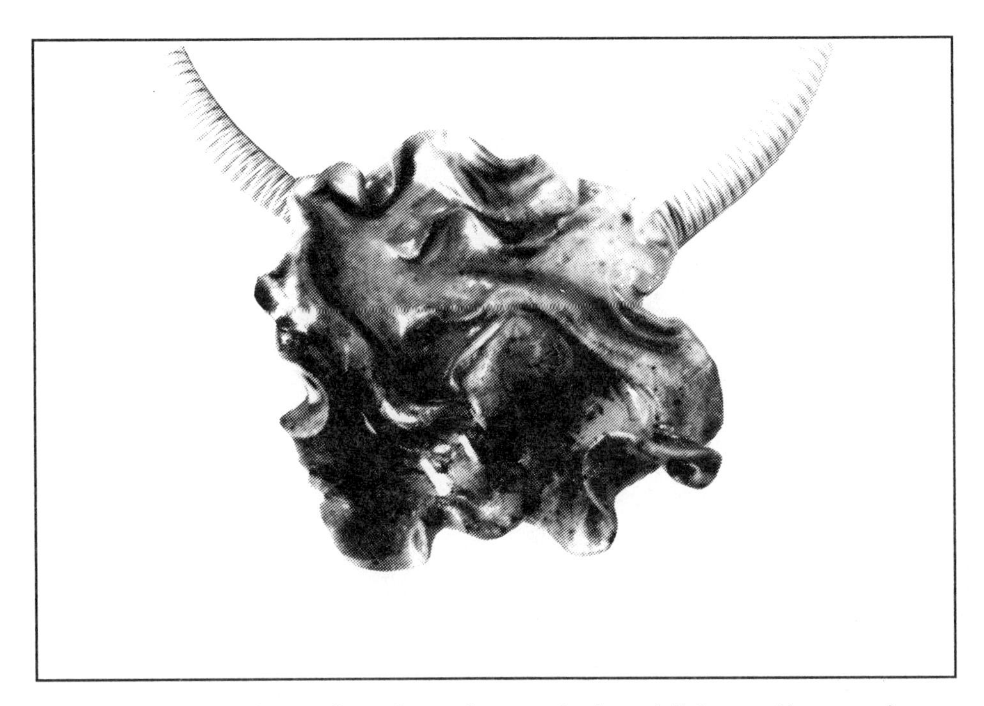

This necklace is such a free form abstract it is pretty much up to you to determine what shape it will take. Using white or neutral colored compound roll it to about 1/8" thick and cut a free form shape from it. You may use Pattern N8 as a guide if you care to. Then press the ends a bit thinner and begin to press parts up and stretch some parts down – and twist. Use photograph as a guide.

Fire at 225° for 15-20 minutes. Color is made by rubbing in **Dr. Ph. Martins** concentrated water color. Mix a drop or two of any colors you care to use with a little bit of water and spread with a brush or your finger. Spray or glaze after color is dry.

The cord is made by wrapping soutache tightly around an ordinary upholstery cord. Glue bullet fasteners on to each end and attach two jump rings and a hook catch.

Necklace N9

This necklace is a beautiful red poinsettia. Using the method described on the following page you can make all types of similar flowers.

The cord on this one is 5 strands of green silk cording fastened with two bell-shaped fasteners, two jump rings and a hook clasp.

ANOTHER COLORFUL IDEA! SEE COLOR PHOTO P.114

Necklace N9, continued

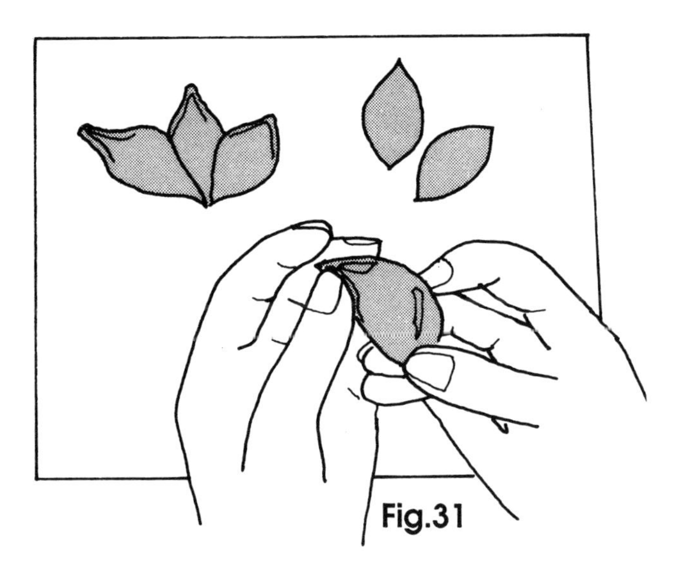

Fig.31

After rolling out white or red compound about 1/8" thick, cut out the pattern pieces. Shape as in illustration. **Fig.31**

After shaping all pieces, fit the 6 biggest pieces together as in **Fig.32** Blend together in the middle.

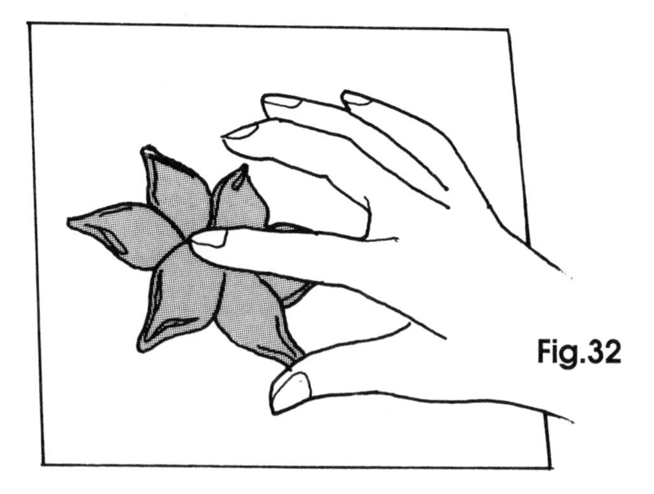

Fig.32

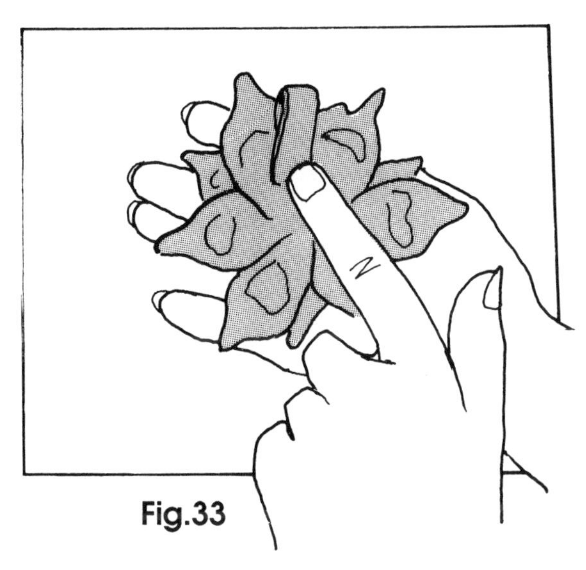

Fig.33

One by one put the 6 medium pieces on top of these (see photos) Blend these in the middle also. Do the same with the 4 small ones. Then make a loop on the back near the top to accomodate the cord. **Fig.33**

For the center press a small amount of the compound through the extruder, using the die with medium holes. Fit this in the center and then fire to 225° for about 20 minutes. The center will not be secure after firing, so glue it in place. Paint the leaves with red acrylic paint and the center in green. **Fig.34**

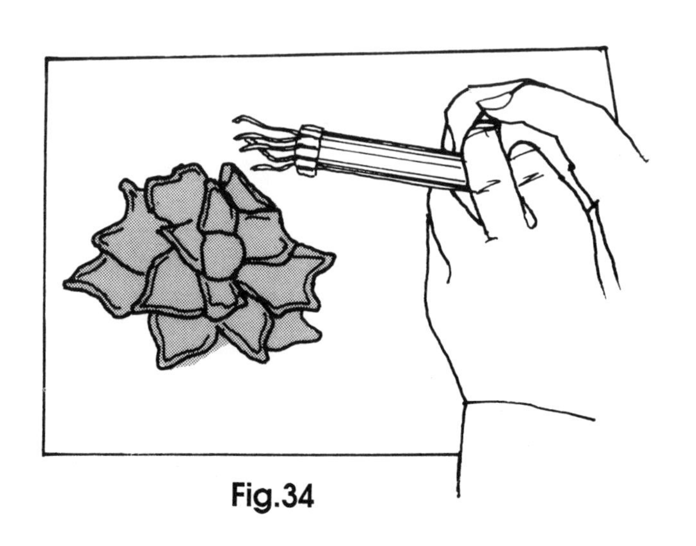

Fig.34

Necklace N10

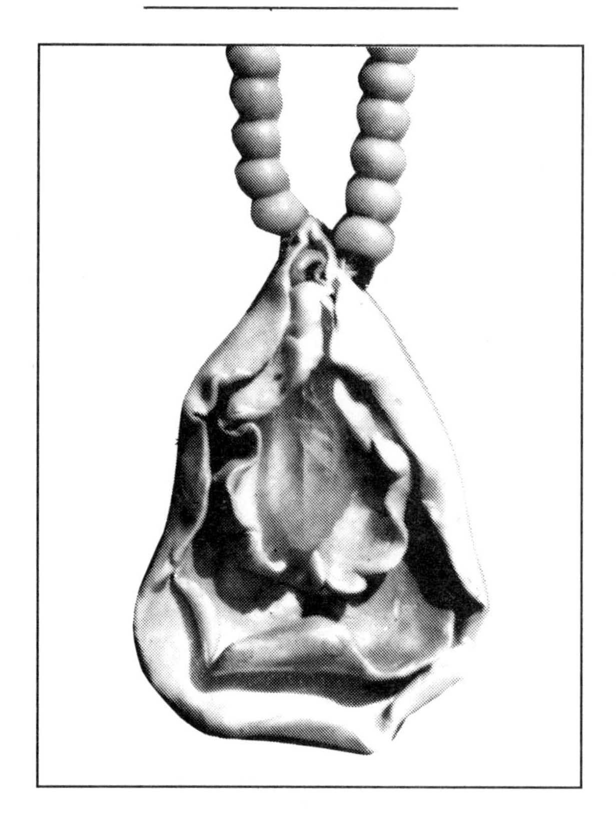

This necklace has a crystal in the center. The shape of the necklace depends mainly on the shape of your crystal. It is made from white compound and colored with pearlized eye shadow and fine glitter. Three cords are strung through the top and it is fastened with 2 bell shaped fasteners, 2 jump rings and a hook fastener.

TWO OTHER INTERESTING IDEAS!

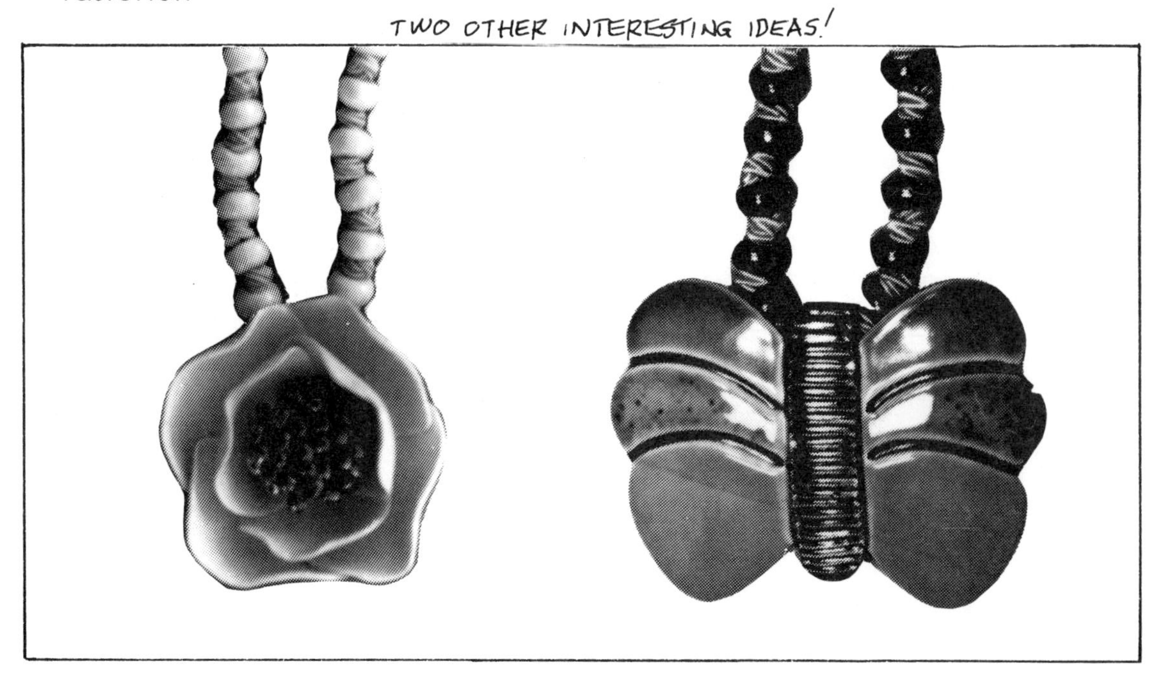

Necklace N10, continued

You need a long crystal, a 2 1/2 oz. white Sculpey, pearlized eye shadow or stains and irredescent fine glitter.

After rolling out compound about 1/8" thick, cut out the pattern pieces.

Rub stains or eyeshadow into all pieces until you get the effect you want. Sprinkle and press into all the pieces the variegated glitter. Then shape the large piece and ruffle as in **Fig.35.**

Do the same with the medium-sized pieces. Then fit the medium-sized ones into the large one.

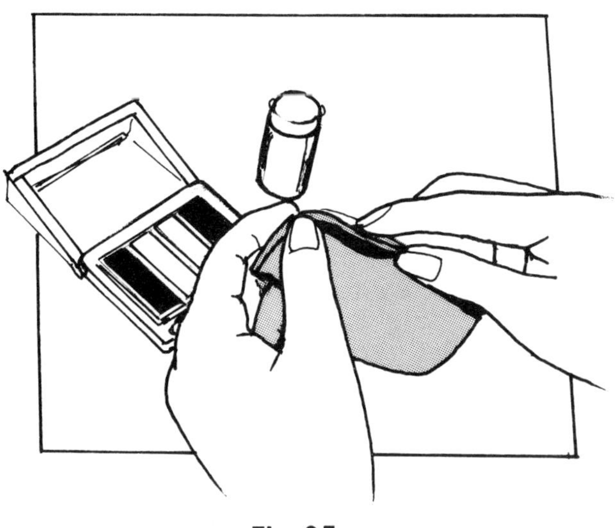

Fig.35

Place crystal on small oval and ruffle around edges. Fit this into the other piece, then press together at the top and put a hole through as shown in **Fig.36**

Fire (with crystal in place) to 225° for 20 minutes. After firing, if the crystal and other pieces seem a little loose, put epoxy around them. This adds to the overall shiny effect, but let it dry before putting it on the cord.

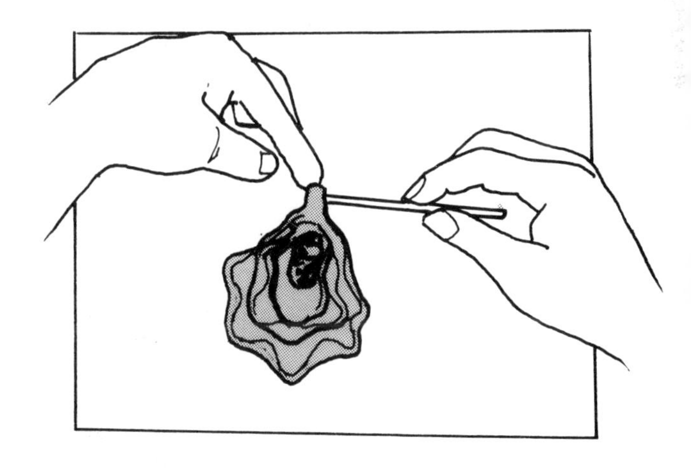

Fig.36

Necklace N11

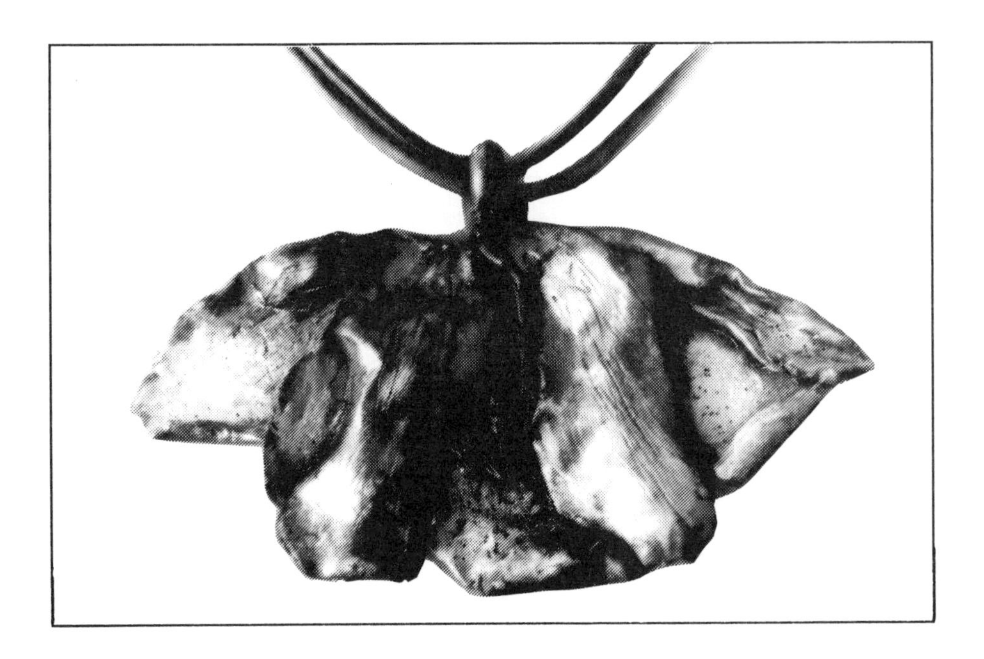

This is one of the most beautiful necklaces. It is modeled after Dogwood. A Dogwood blossom was picked and allowed to dry out, then used as a model to form the petals. The pistil was made from a small roll of compound and some copper wires. Five cords were put through the loop and fastened in back with two bullet fasteners, two jump rings and an adjustable hook.

Necklace N11, continued

Use about 2 1/2 oz. of white compound and a tiny bit of brown. White and beige color eyeshadows or stains.

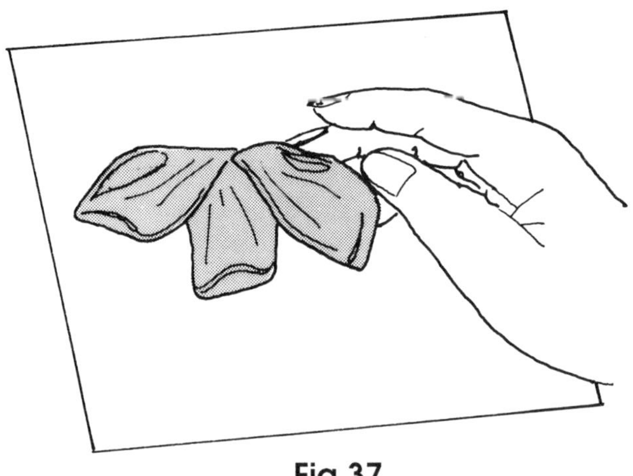

Fig.37

Soften and roll out the compound to about 1/8" thick. Rub white and beige stains or eyeshadows into each piece. With a needle (or pointed tool) scratch lines into them for veins. Sprinkle bronze powder on a few spots. Then ruffle and turn out edges as shown in photograph. Place three together **(Fig.37).**

Place the other two on top, overlapping the others. Press the top of them together. Then roll a small tube and form it into a loop with a pencil. Blend this into the back as shown in **(Fig.38)**

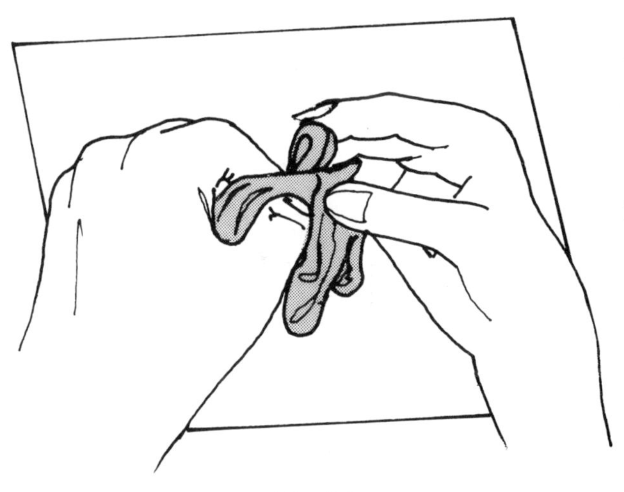

Fig.38

For the pistil make a small roll with the brown. Cut a few copper wires and pinch these together at the top. Place in the middle of the flower a bit under the petals. **(Fig.39)**

Poke a few holes in the pistil with a needle. Fire at 250° for 20 minutes. When cool spray with a matt finish.

Fig.39

Necklace N12

This is just one of a series of "pebbles" as the artist calls them.

Make 5 irregular "pebbles" out of Super Sculpey. Keep them flat on the back. Press any color stones you have into them (see picture). Wrap copper wire around the pebbles until you get a nice effect. Rub brass, gold and copper powder into them. See "Things That Are Fun to Experiment With", page 86.
Press glitter on until you get the effect you like. Put holes in. Line the pieces up the way you will expect to string them – largest at center, etc. Make holes large enough for cord you wish to use. Fire at 250° for 30 minutes or until you see them darkening.

When cool you may add a bit of white nail polish here and there. The epoxy recommended in this book may be used on the top surfaces for a shiny effect. It also holds the stones more securely. The secret of the interesting look of these is using the Super Sculpey and firing it *longer* until it has a rich dark look. Be sure to have enough ventilation in your studio when firing as well as when spraying or gluing.

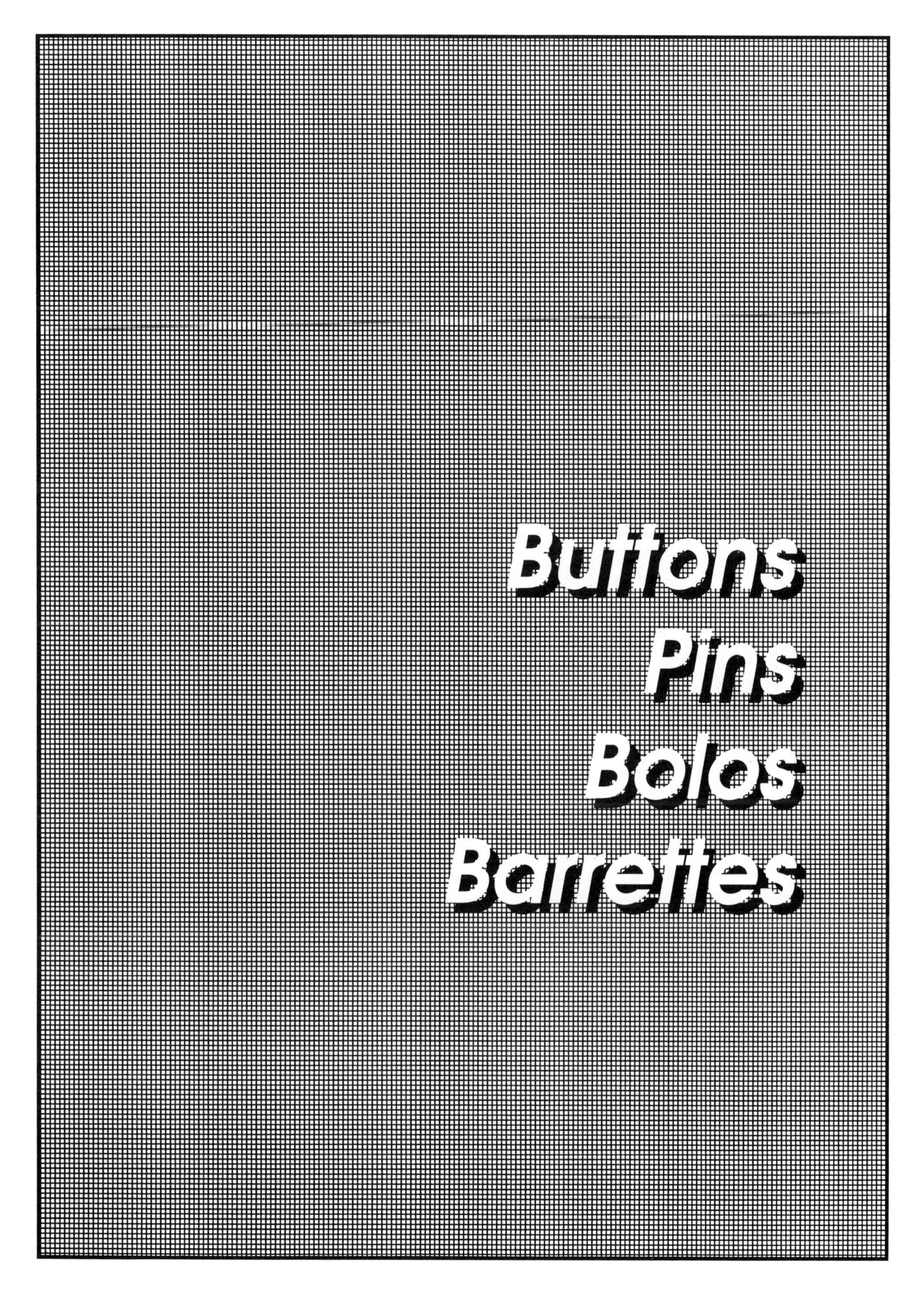
Buttons
Pins
Bolos
Barrettes

BUTTONS, PINS, BOLOS, BARRETTES

The following pages refer to the color plate of each piece with a brief description of each and how to make them. The directions are very brief as the methods have already been explained in detail in this book.

However, here are a few special things to remember when making them.

1. When several pieces are placed on top of one another, they will not adhere in firing unless they are securely fastened around the edge. A bit of glue may be used to fasten them after firing.
2. Eyeshadows, stains, Gold or Silver Bronze Pulver, glass and stones may be fired on a piece. Paints and nail polishes can only be used <u>after</u> firing.
3. Fire the barrettes on the barrette fastener so it will keep the contour of the fastener.
4. A glaze was sprayed or brushed on all the pieces to give a more finished look and to more securely hold any added decorations.
5. All the buttons have two holes in them for sewing onto your garment. As alternates you may choose to put a little extra compound on the back with a hole through it or glue on a button back (see No. F12 on **Fastener** page).
6. Refer to color pictures on pages 3,4,113 and 114 when making these as there are no patterns for buttons, pins, bolos or fasteners.

BUTTONS • BT series

See color page 114. Numbers start in upper left hand corner and go across.

BT 1	This is a simple marbleized button. Colors used are blue, green, yellow, white and metallic bronze around the outside.
BT 2	A flower button – made from white with a blue metallic eye-shadow rubbed in – with a little gold on the edges. Purple metallic compound is used in the center with touches of gold. Rub and buff on top.
BT 3	For this round button a green compound was used. A fern was pressed into it and while still in place, Gold Bronze Pulver was rubbed on the parts not covered with the fern pattern. A little lined texture was put around the edges.
BT 4	Black compound was used with pearlized compound around a piece of abalone shell. Four tiny pearls were pressed into the top and bottom.
BT 5	A round black button with bits of green, pink, red and blue compound pressed in. Lines were drawn around the outside with a gold caligraphic pen.
BT 6	Yellow and white marbleized compound was put on a larger white disc. Texture was put around disc.
BT 7	Use a light compound for the background, put tiny balls on for flowers. Roll in thin tubes of green for leaves. Press in centers with a ball point pen.
BT 8	Metallic bronze was used with a glass nugget in the center. Tiny blue beads were pressed in each corner and a lined design drawn on.
BT 9	A little half circle design of metallic gray was pressed on a circle of the same color. Tiny pearls were pressed in around the edge of the design. Rose nail polish was painted on the raised part and to create texture on the other half a round pointed stick was pressed into it.
BT 10	Brown compound was rolled and cut into a small egg shape. White compound was pushed through the small extruder. The "strings" were pressed on the lower half and gold stain was rubbed on them.

BUTTONS • BT series, continued

BT 11	A simple flower button was made by extruding blue compound and pressing it onto a small circle. A white ball was put in the middle and textured with a pin point.
BT 12	Cut an oval shape from gray compound. Place small balls in center as shown in picture – and little oblong rolls around for leaves. Press balls in center with an old ball point pen. Make leaf designs on the oblongs.
BT 13	This flower design is cut out of white. Lines are scratched in. A white pearlized eyeshadow is rubbed on the top. Tiny balls are put in center. With a ball point pen press in center. Then rub gold on them.
BT 14	Marbleized colors of your choice. Roll and cut an odd circle and ruffle.
BT 15	Cut an egg shape from bright green. Marbleize orange, green and yellow. Roll and cut into a small egg shape. Press on top.

MORE BUTTON DESIGNS

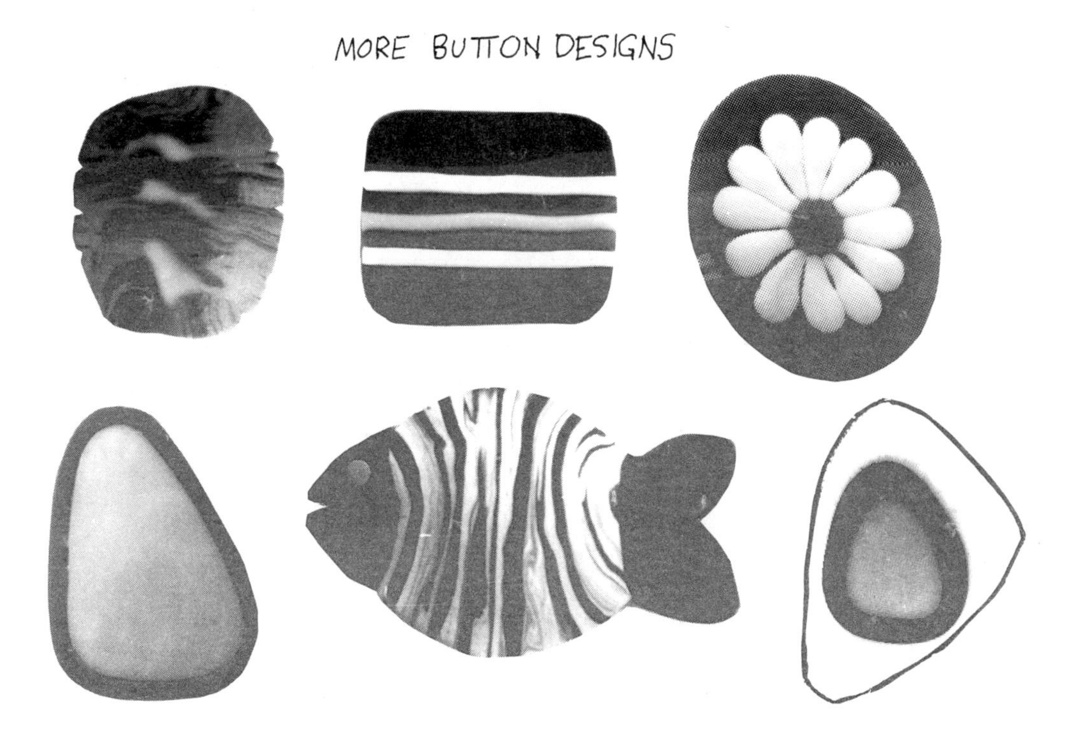

PINS • P series

See color page 4. Numbers start in upper left hand corner and go across.

This pin is made from white compound rolled rather thin. A piece of black celophane ribbon with holes is pressed on top. Different color /s are rubbed in until you get the effect that you like. a thin glaze is applied to better secure the ribbon.

---

hite compounds are marbleized and rolled thin for this ›wer.It is cut into various length strips and they are placed nother as in the photographs. A ball of pink is used for the ıe flower.

---

apes are cut from rolled light color compound. Rub some on some ends and gold on the rest. Fit them together as in oh.

---

rple, blue and black were marbleized, rolled 1/8 inch thin ı the shape of a butterfly. The center piece is cut then th Gold Bronze Pulver and pressed on. It may have to be after firing unless you secure the sides well.

---

pin is made from a lace design. A light compound is rolled ınd rubbed with a rose blush (or stain). Then the lace design on. The high parts are rubbed with Gold Pulver. Remove then fire.

---

dd shape from any rolled light colored compound. After k and green acrylic paints are brushed on. A lttle glitter is on before the paint is dry.

---

abstract shape with 6 thin strips of bronze compound

---

pin made with five marbleized petal shapes and a enter

BOLOS • BL series

page 113. Numbers start in upper left hand corner and go across.

'ellow shape is placed on a gray yellow and red marbleized hey are then placed on a larger red shape. After firing the ıre glued. A bolo fastener is glued on the back.

PAGE 79
color page for PINS should read page 113
color page for BOLOS should read page 4
PAGE 80
color page for BARRETTES should read page 4

BOLOS • BL series, continued

BL 2	This simple little shape is just a gray, green, yellow and orange marbleized piece with a bolo fastener glued on the back.
BL 3	A fun bird. Make feathers from Super Sculpey. Put the lines in and brush the high spots with silver buff. Fire them separately from the body part at a higher temperature to darken the lines. Make the body from any color you choose to. Fire, and glue on feather piece as shown in photo.
BL 4	This bolo is made like one of the necklaces (N8). It is simply an abstract shape cut from rolled compound with different stains, paints or eyeshadows rubbed in. It is then curved up and ruffled.

MORE PINS

See Color page 4 (bottom 2)

P 9	These three little stick pins are nice to wear on lapels.
P 10	This is a red poinsettia made like Necklace N9.

BARRETTES • BR series

(see color page 113)

BR 1	This is marbleized green, yellow, black and orange piece glued on a light colored piece that has been rubbed with Gold Bronze Pulver. Fire these barrettes on the barrette fastener so that they remain curved. It will fit the contour of the barrette fastener better when it is glued on.
BR 2	Bronze compound is used for the background of this barrette. Lines are made around the edge by rolling on it a cap with lines on it. You will find these on a lot of tooth-paste tubes and other tubes you have around the house. The center part is very interesting – it is a dark colored piece of compound rolled in all types of glitter. A light glaze is used after firing to fix them more permanently. Fire this piece on a barrette fastener to maintain the curvature.

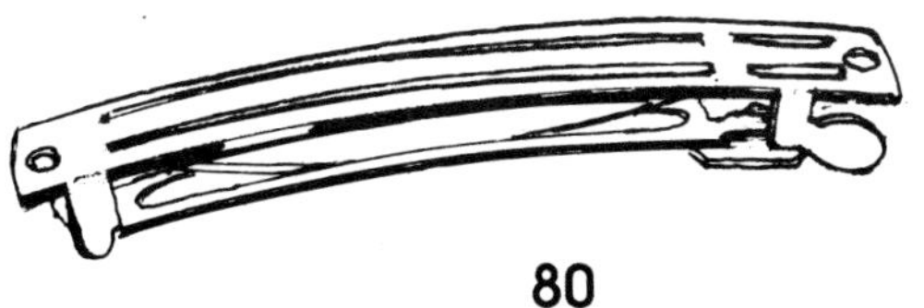

Barrette holder

Fasteners

FASTENERS

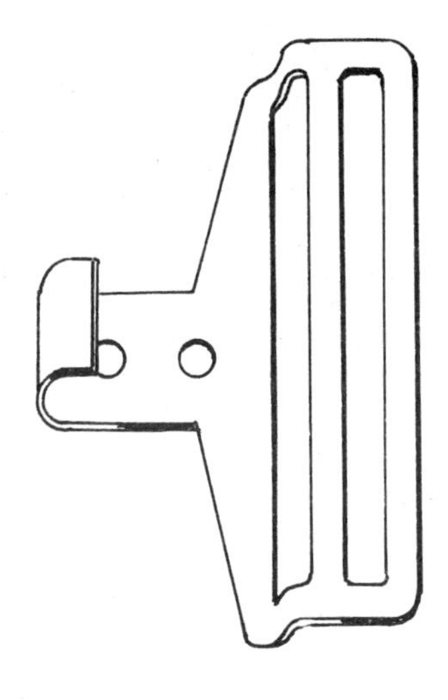

No. F1. Adjustable Belt Fastener

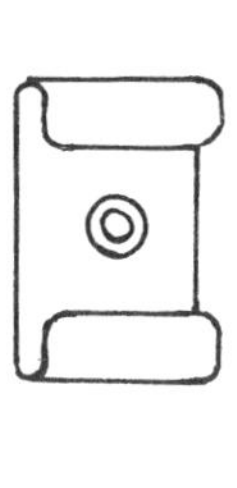

No. F2. Belt connector for gluing

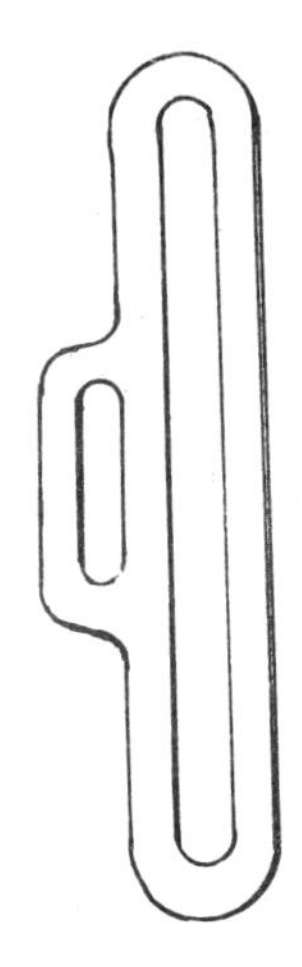

No. F3. Belt Eye

No. F4. Adjustable Necklace Hook

NO. F5. Jump Ring

No. F6. Clamping Fastener to use on both ends of cord to fasten jump rings and hook

No. F7. Earring clip with plastic back for gluing

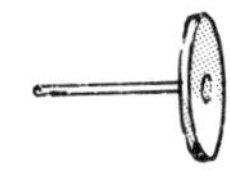

No. F8. Flat Post for pierced ear.

No. F9. Clutch

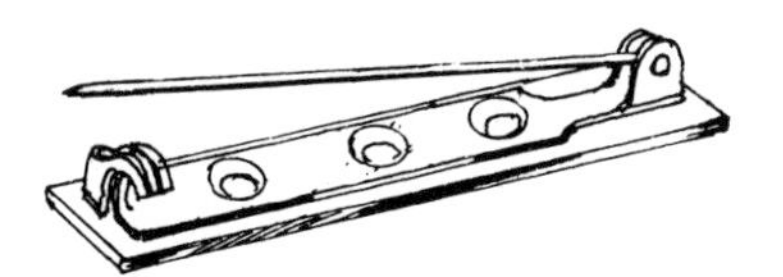

No. F10. Pin Back

No. F11. Bolo Fastener

No. F12. Button Back

FASTENERS

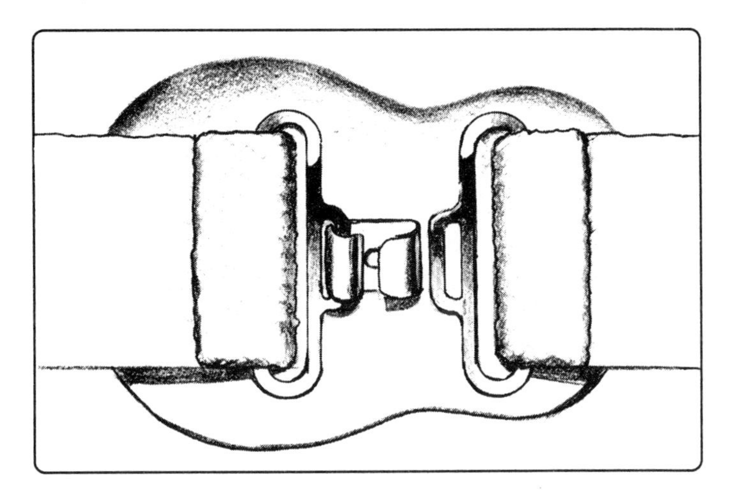

For all stretch belts a No.F2 connector is glued on the back of the buckle. A No. F3 Belt Eye is sewed on each end of the stretch belt as illustrated. To make the buckle more secure put it on a soft surface and with the eye in place press down one side.

To make a belt similar to that shown on Buckle B5 no fasteners are required.

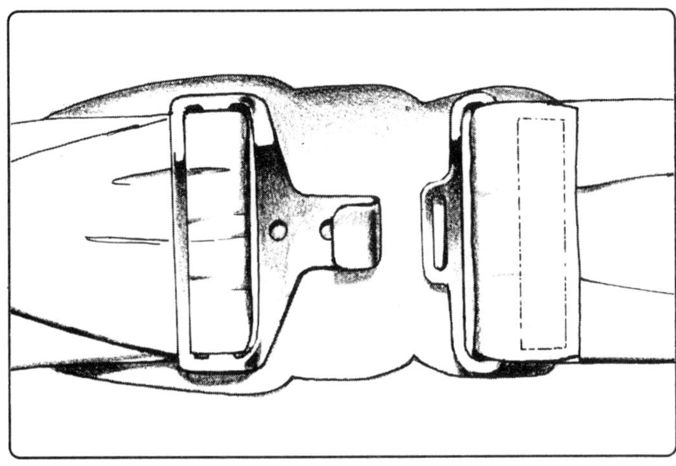

For leather, suede and other non-stretch materials a No.F1 adjustable fastener is glued on the back of the buckle. A No.F3 Belt Eye is sewed on one end of the belt. The other end is tapered to slide through the loop. See illustration at left.

Necklaces

Use a Clamping Fastener No. F6 with Jump Ring No. F5 and an adjustable Hook No F4 for connecting necklaces with beads. On others you may want a cord you can tie around your neck. Use 3 strands for this. Make them longer than you want the finished piece to look so that you can braid the ends after beads and and pendant are slipped on.(See **SOURCES** for fasteners).

Gluing

EnviroTex 1 to 1 Polymer Coating is good to use for gluing backs on finished pieces. Spread the polymer coating on the back of the piece, put on the fastener and then put more coating on top of that part of the fastener that touches the polyform compound.

Earrings, Pins, Bolos and Buttons

Select the proper fastener for your design and follow the same directions as above.

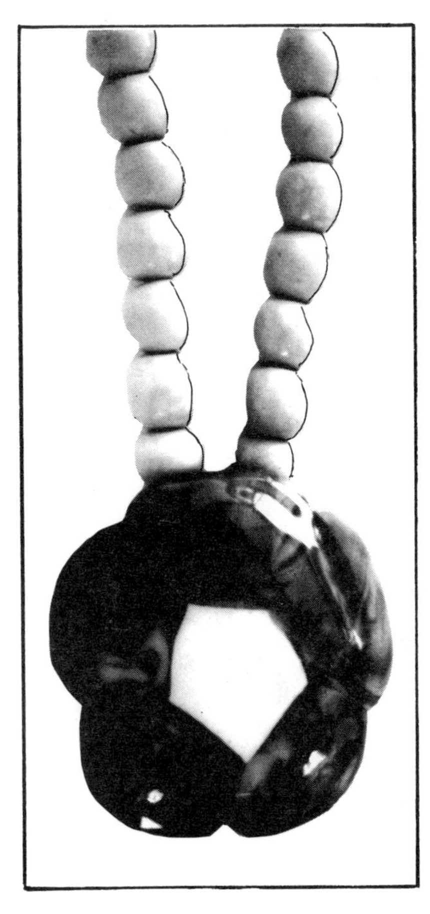

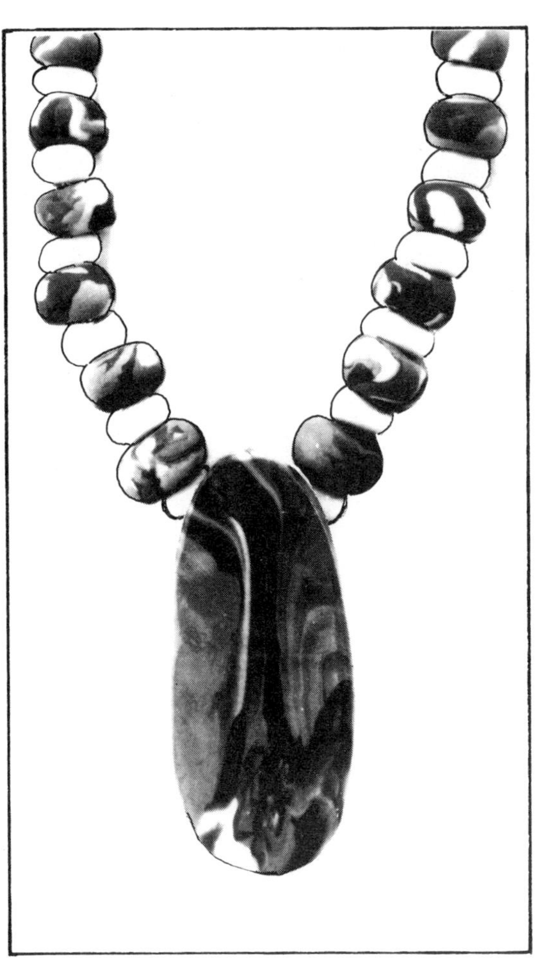

MORE NECKLACE IDEAS!

Products
Glossary
Special Tips
Sources

Products

The following are some of the products that work very well on modeling compounds:

Spray Glazes

1. **Accent Polyurethane –** satin finish made by the Illinois Bronze Paint Co., Lake Zurich, IL 60047.
2. **The Original Treasurer Sealer –** a clear vinyl spray. Made by Plaid Enter–prise, Inc. Norcross, GA 30091.
3. **Model Master.** A clear lacquer semi-gloss made by the Testor Corporation, Rockford, IL 61104.
4. All the modeling compound brands have a glaze they sell with their product.
5. Any other acrylic glazes

Products for Coloring

1. **Acrylic paints** – obtained from your art store
2. **Rub 'n Buff** – all shades (especially silver and gold). Craft shops.
3. **Silber Pulver** by Eberhard Faber – a fine powdered glitter – bronze, copper and gold.
4. **Prisma Glitter** by Gick Publishing, Inc. A salt-like glitter in colors.
5. **Dr. Ph. Martin's** concentrated water colors. Dilute a drop or two with water and brush on fired piece. Obtained at your art store.

Glue

1. **EnviroTex.** 1 to 1 polymer coating. Get this at your crafts shop. It may also be used to seal in stones, wires, etc., you may want to use to decorate some pieces.

Things that are fun to experiment with

1. **Copper wire** – at your hardware.
2. **Eyeshadows** – purchase at discount store where it is less expensive.
3. **Nail polish** – all different shades – pearlized ones are good.
4. **Shells** – at shops that sell nature items.
5. **All types of stones** – also at your nature shop.

Finally, don't be afraid to try anything. This is the only way you will get interesting, surprising results.

Glossary

Modeling Compound. A polyvinylchloride plastic. There are several brands available. The most popular brands are **Sculpey** and **FIMO.** Most of the designs in this book were done with these two brands. Some call these compounds "clay", but even though it has the modeling consistency of clay, it is not clay or ceramic. Among the advantages over clay: (1) It does not need a lot of equipment, (2) does not dry out if left uncovered and (3) there are a varicty of colors.

Glaze. Lacquer or acrylic for brushing or spraying on your piece after firing to obtain a matt or shiny finish.

Firing. The term we use for baking in your oven.

Blending. Mixing two or more colors together to get one solid color.

Knead. Mixing like you would bread dough until soft or blended.

Marbleize. Mixing two or more colors together enough so there are streaks of different colors throughout.

Special Tips

1. Keep a bottle of hand lotion handy. Rub into your hands before starting to soften the compound. Use it also to clean hands each time you work with a new color. Wipe off with paper toweling or a cloth.
2. Be sure to have ventilation in your area when firing or spraying glazes.
3. Remember you can use **Envirotex** 1 to 1 Polymer Coating as a glaze as well as for gluing.
4. On buckles be sure to curve them to fit around waist in front and put a long piece of the compound under it when firing to keep it a bit curved.
5. Don't hesitate to mix with your polymer pieces any beads you buy at a bead shop or even things you can find at hardware stores. There are a lot of little nuts, bolts and copper wire available.

SOURCES

AXNER
435 Aulin Avenue •P.O.Box 1484
Orlando, FL • 32765
(407) 365-2600 or 1-800-843-7057

Modeling compound, belt fasteners, jewelry findings, etc., Belting. Send or call for free catalog.

Rings and Things
W. 814 Main Avenue •P.O.Box 450
Spokane, WA 99210-0450
(509) 624-9565

Very large selection of all types of findings. Send for catalog.

FLAX Art and Design
1699 Market Street • P.O.Box 7216
San Francisco, CA 94120
1-800-547-7778

Art materials, including modeling compounds.

TSI, Inc.
101 Nickerson Street
P.O.Box 9266
Seattle, WA 98109
1-206-282-3040

Findings and modeling materials. Send for catalog.

AFTOSA
1034 Ohio Avenue
Richmond, CA 94804
(415) 233-0334
Outside California - 800-231-0397

Large selection of jewelry findings and modeling compound. Send for catalog.

The Library Store, Inc.
112 E. South Street • P.O.Box 964
Tremont, IL 61508

SCOTCH brand Adhesive Transfer Gun and transfer tape. Send for catalog.

Miami Cork and Supply
10160 N.W. 47th Street
Sunrise, FL 33351
(305) 572-8455

Jewelry supplies, etc., send for catalog.

Fabric Shops

For belting

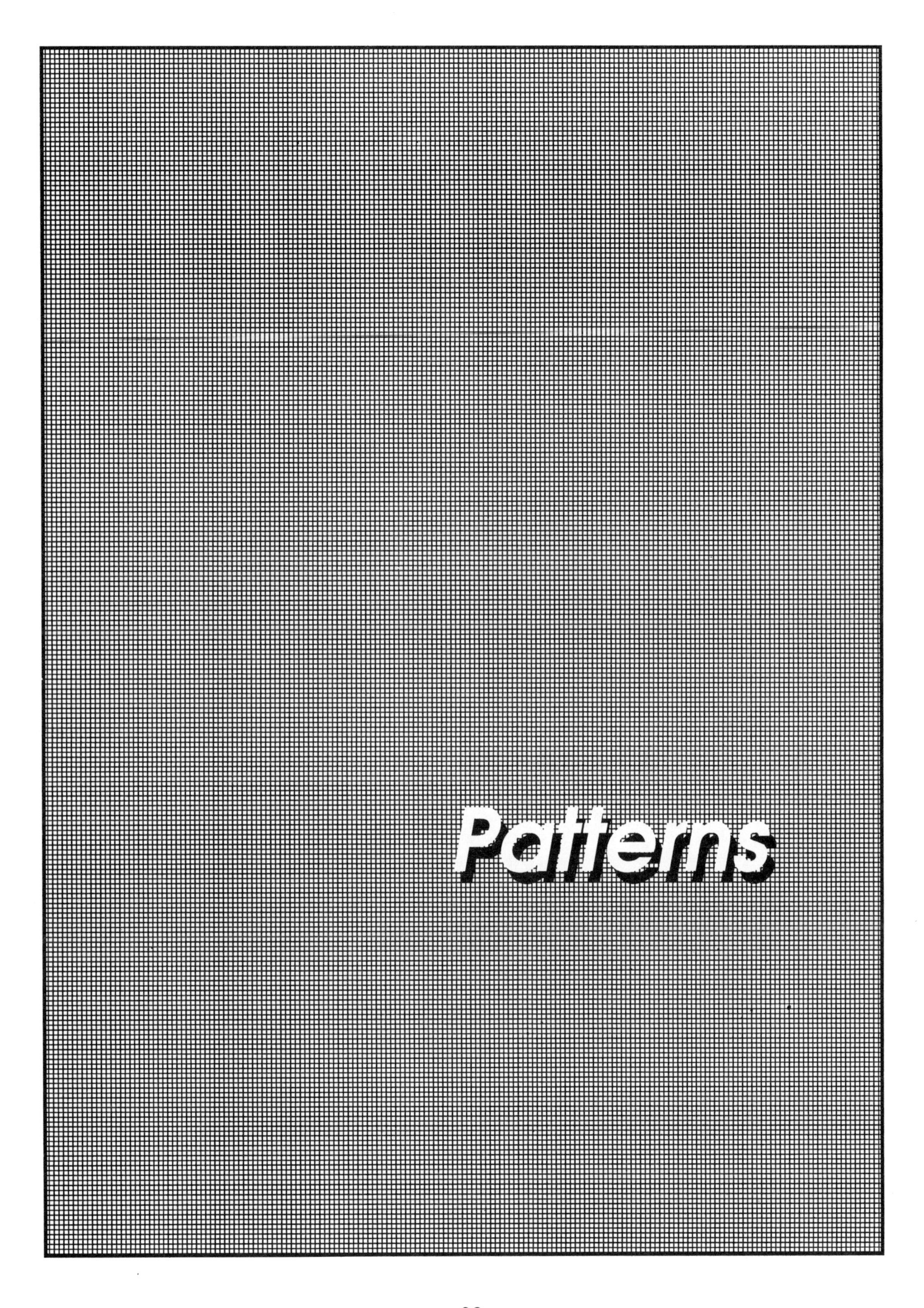
Patterns

Note: for all patterns:

The following patterns may be traced onto something heavier such as cardboard – using carbon paper. Or you may also use a heavy transparent vellum or mylar (using the rough side) to make a direct tracing, then cut out. Then these patterns may be used over and over again.

You may use these patterns exactly as directed or you may experiment and elaborate on them. They can be enlarged, made smaller or reshaped. Let your imagination be your guide. The thinner lines inside the pattern are meant to be traced on the modeling compound. When doing earrings be sure to reverse them for right and/or left when indicated.

- **Buckles are "B" series**
- **Necklaces are "N" series**
- **Pins are "P" series**
- **Earrings are "E" series**
- **Bolos are "BL" series**
- **Buttons are in "BT" series**

PATTERNS FOR BELT BUCKLES AND MATCHING EARRINGS

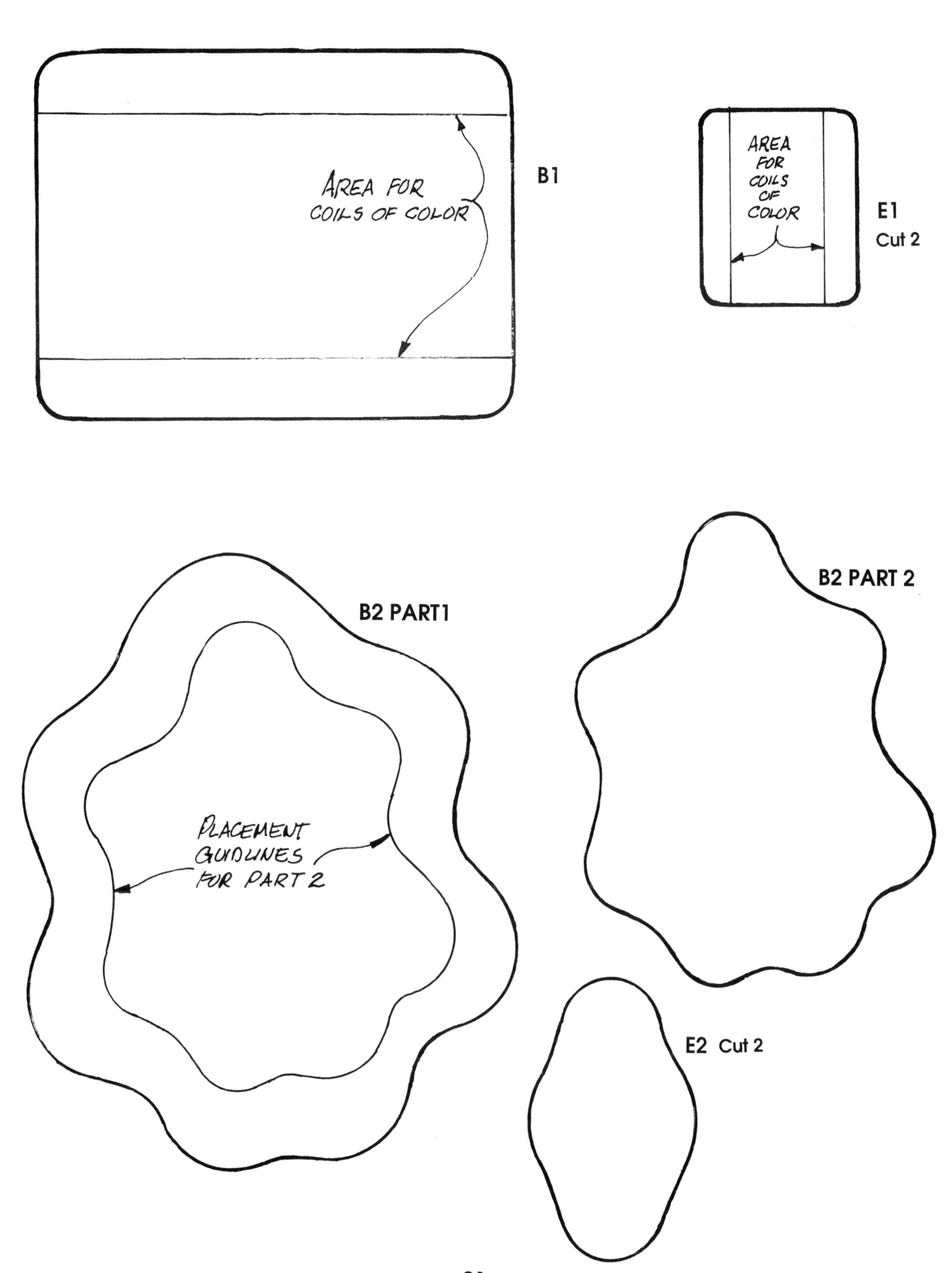

PATTERNS FOR BELT BUCKLES AND MATCHING EARRINGS

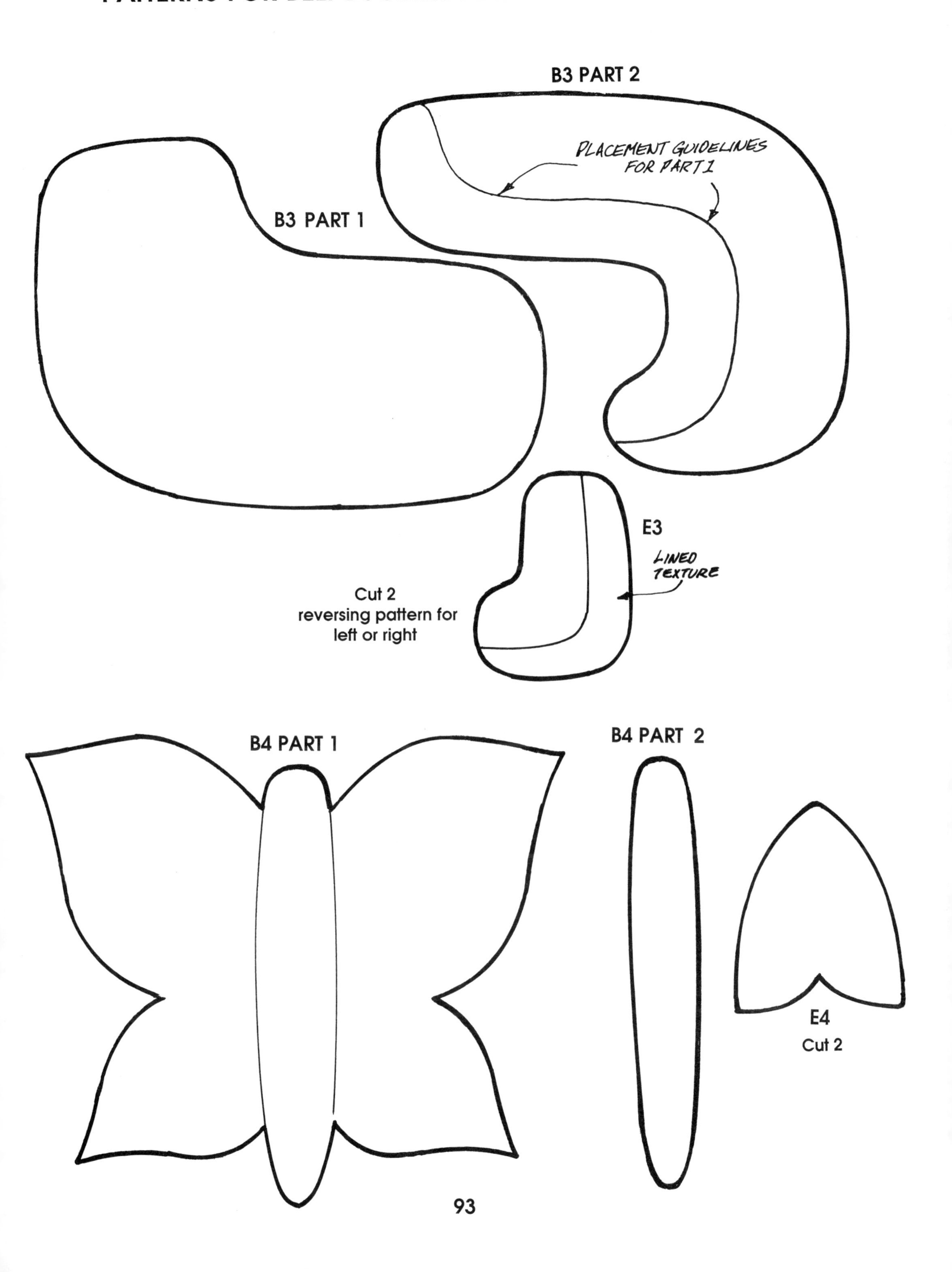

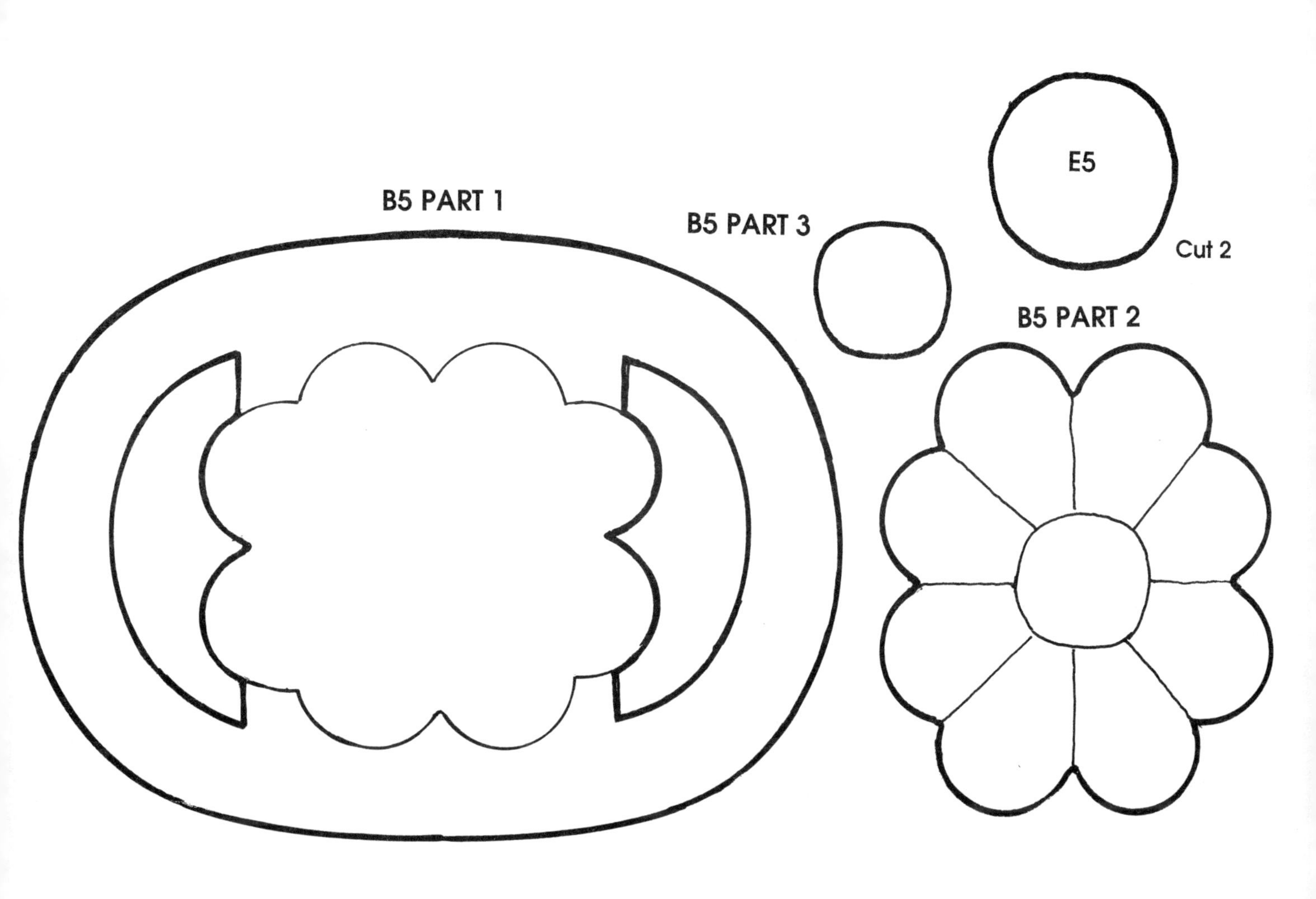

DO EARRINGS
SAME AS ONE FLOWER

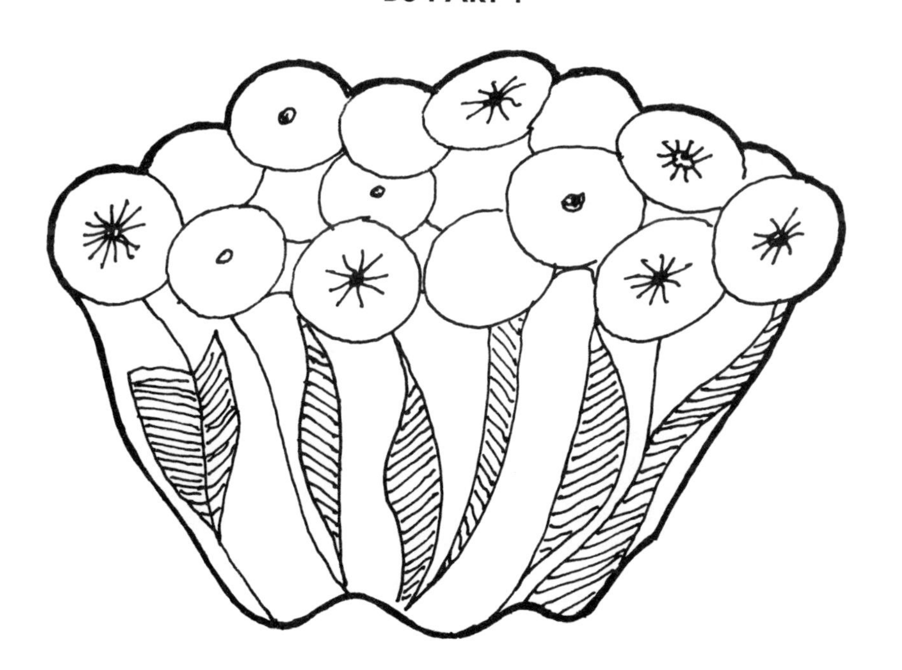

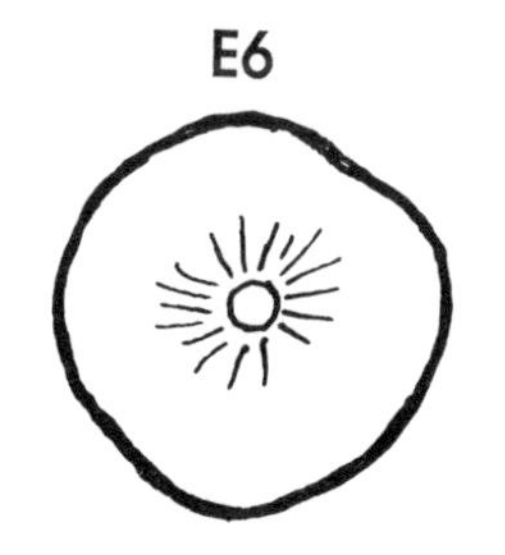

Cut 2
reversing pattern for
left or right

B7

USE THIS PATTERN TO
CUT SHELLFISH EARRINGS

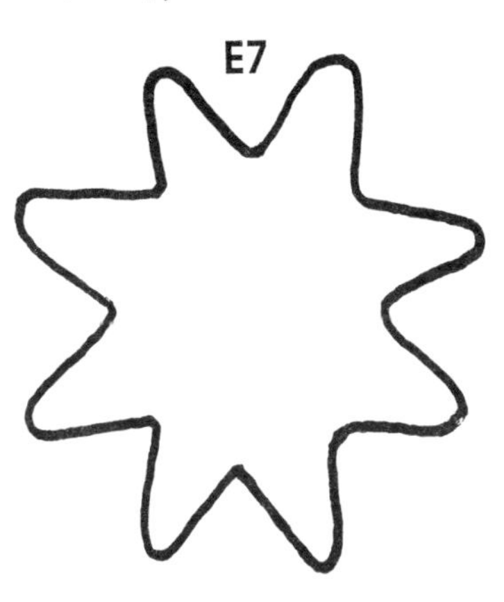

GET A REAL
STARFISH OR USE
THIS FOR PATTERN AND
TEXTURE.
(SEE "TEXTURE" PAGE)

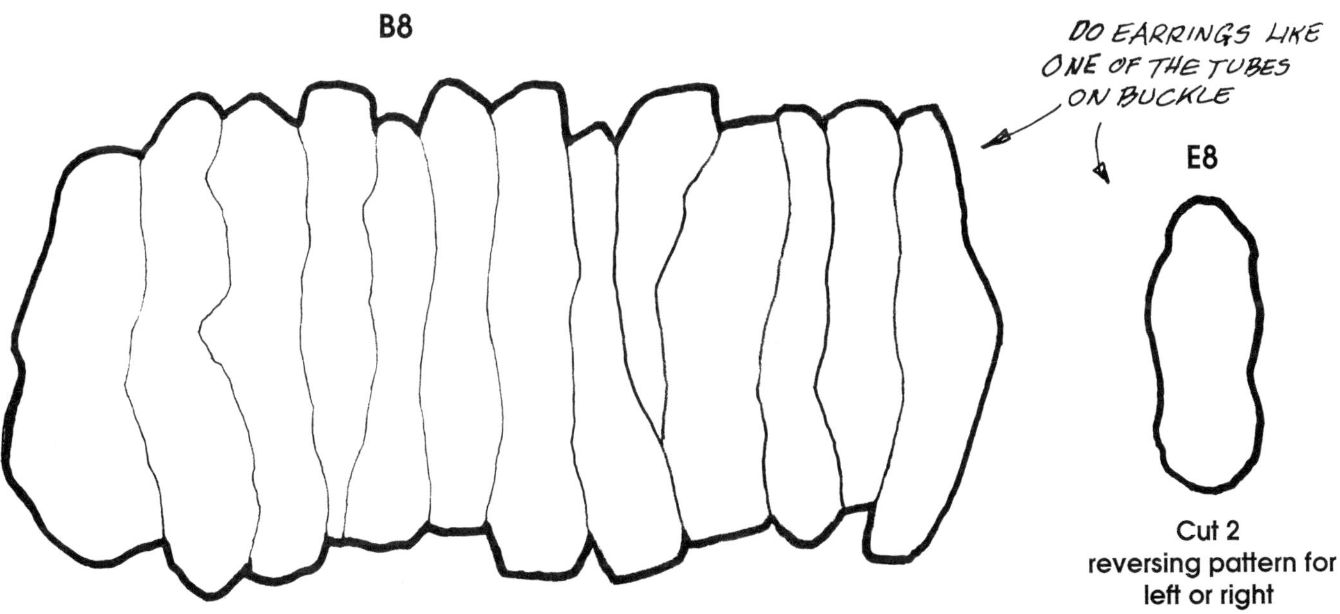

THIS PATTERN IS JUST FOR A GUIDE SINCE BUCKLE
IS MADE FROM TUBES PLACED SIDE-BY-SIDE AND FLATTENED.

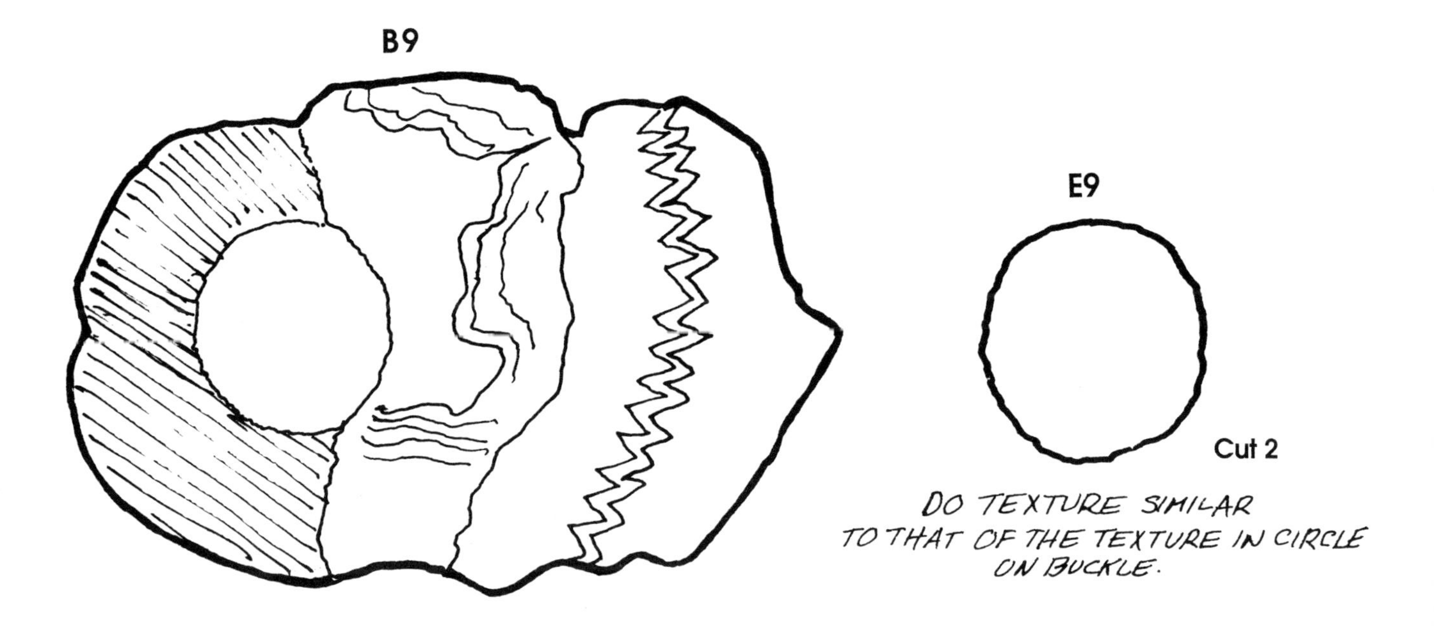
B9
E9
Cut 2
DO TEXTURE SIMILAR
TO THAT OF THE TEXTURE IN CIRCLE
ON BUCKLE.

PATTERNS FOR NECKLACES AND MATCHING EARRINGS

Necklace N1

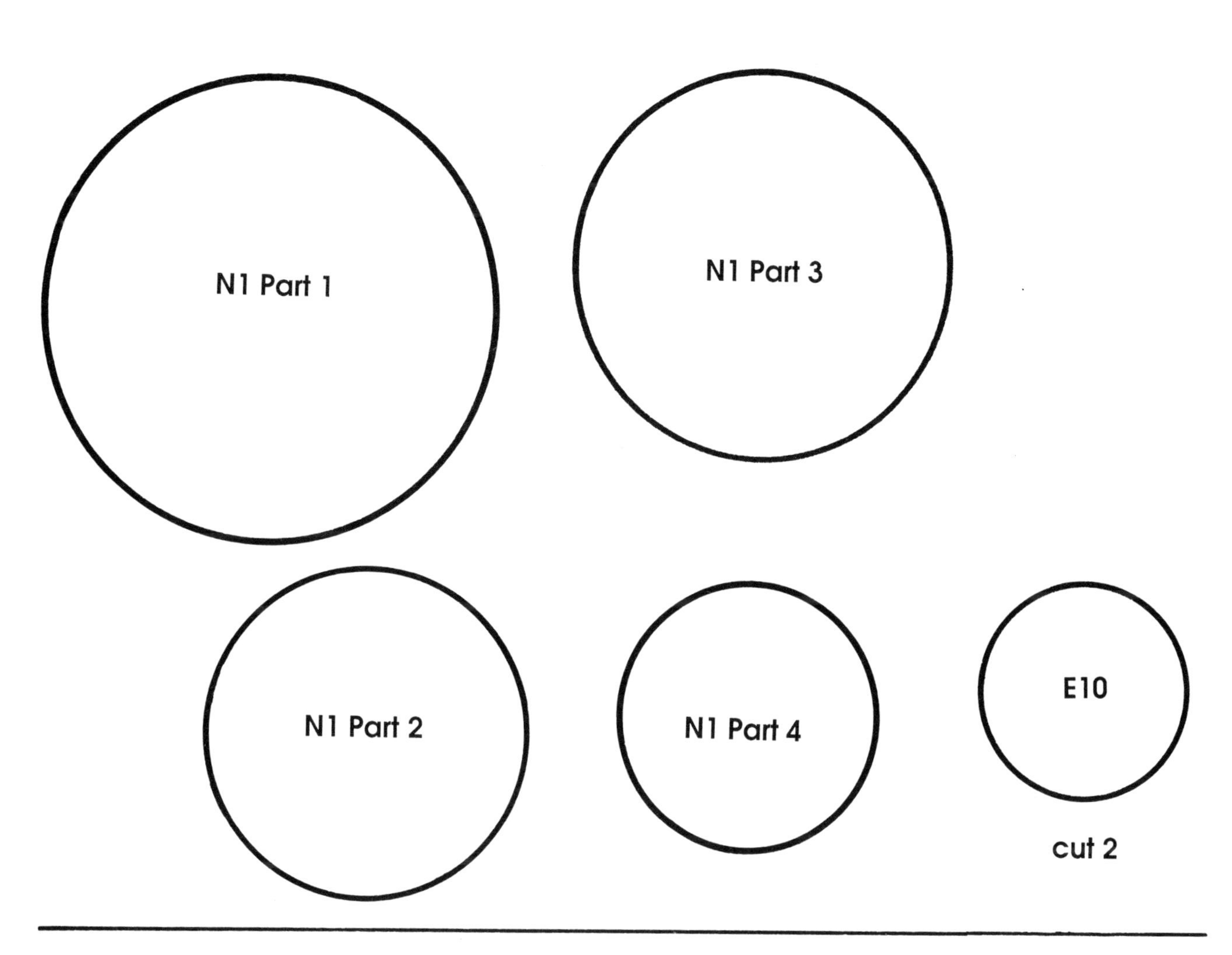

Necklace N2

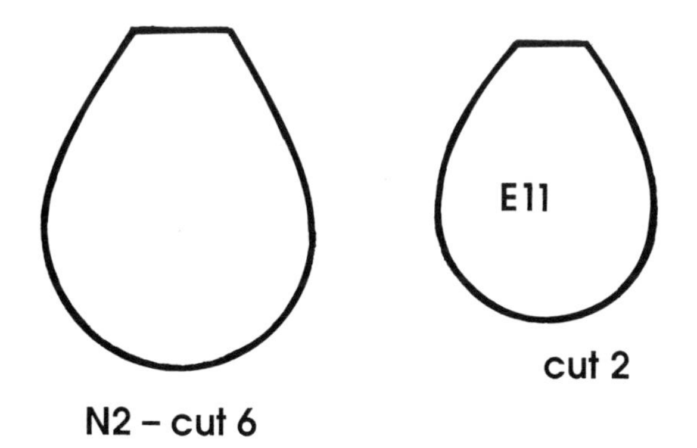

Necklace N3

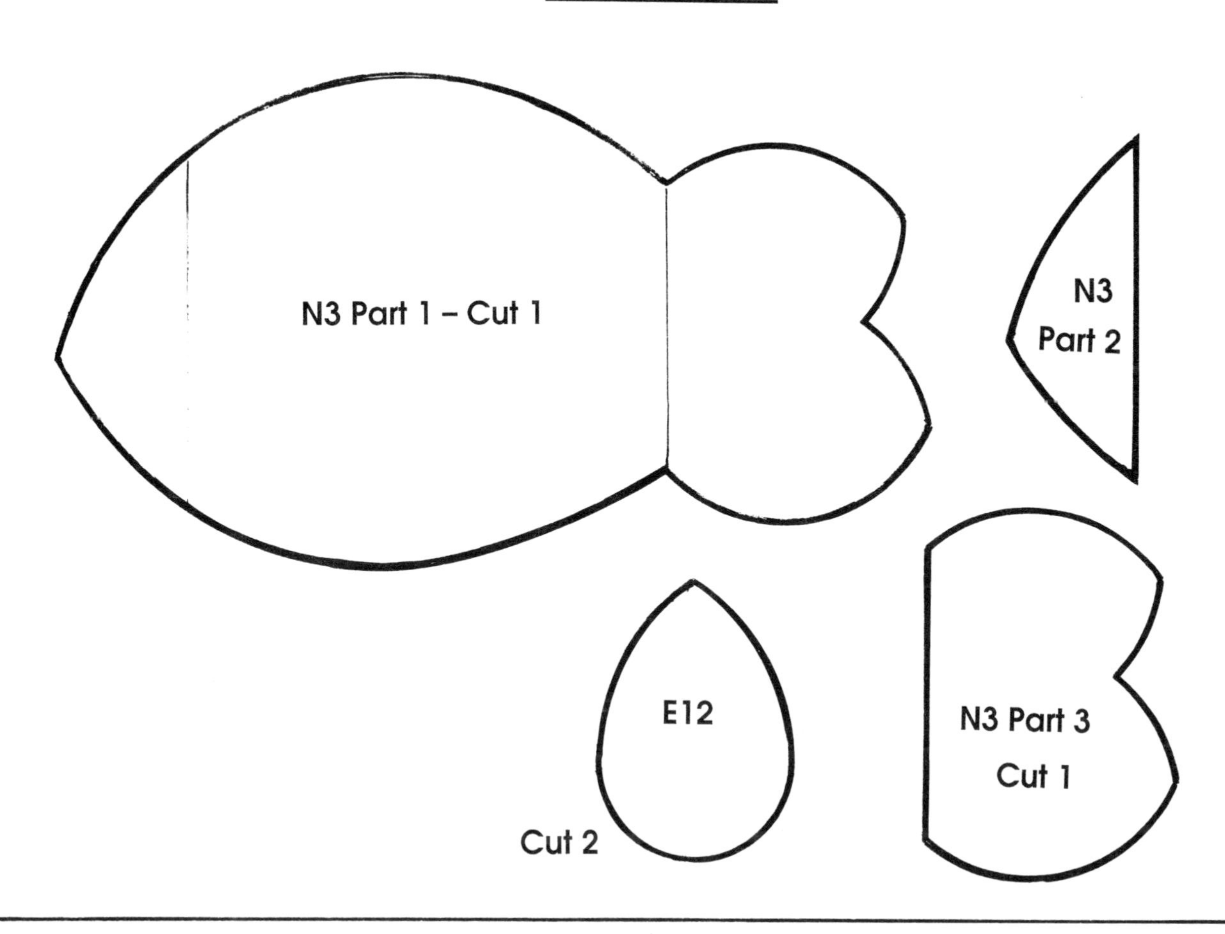

Necklace N4

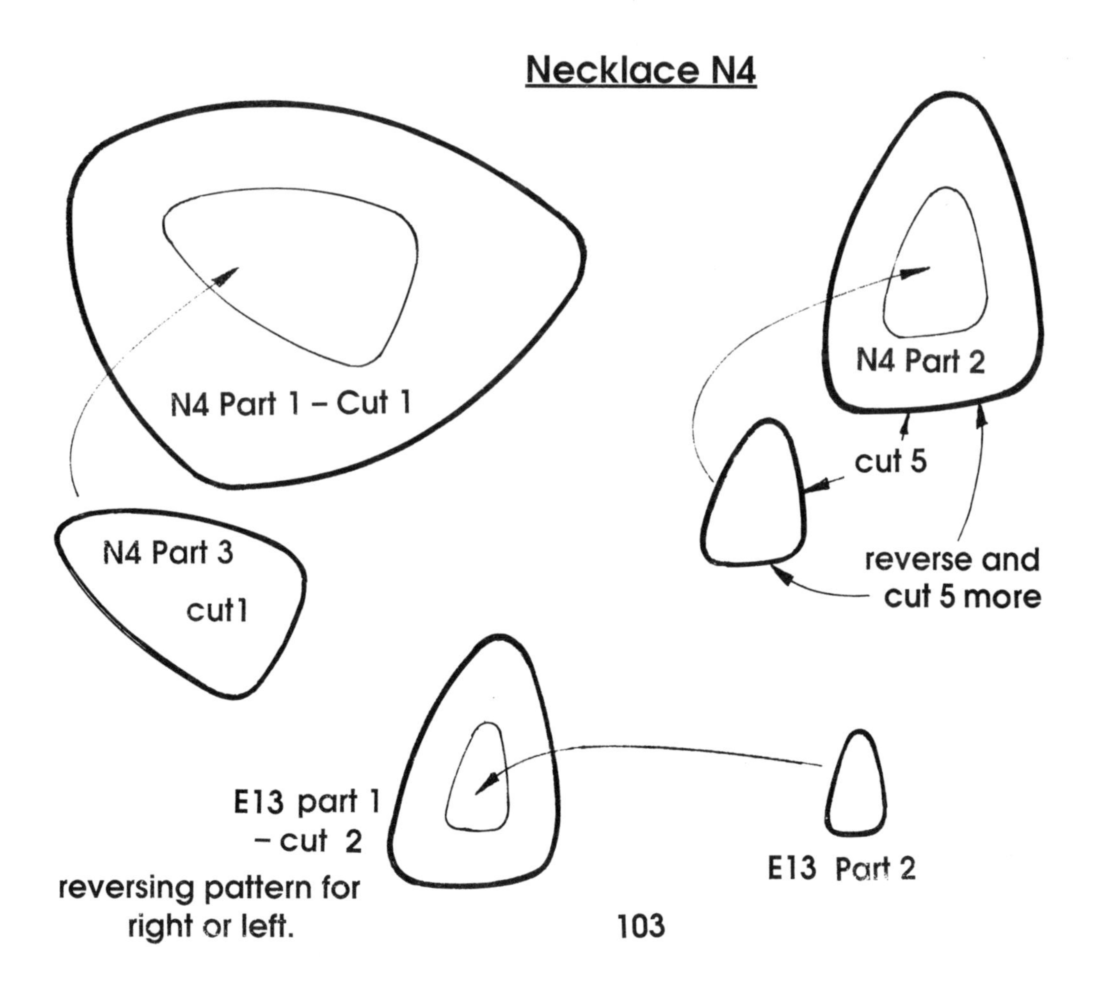

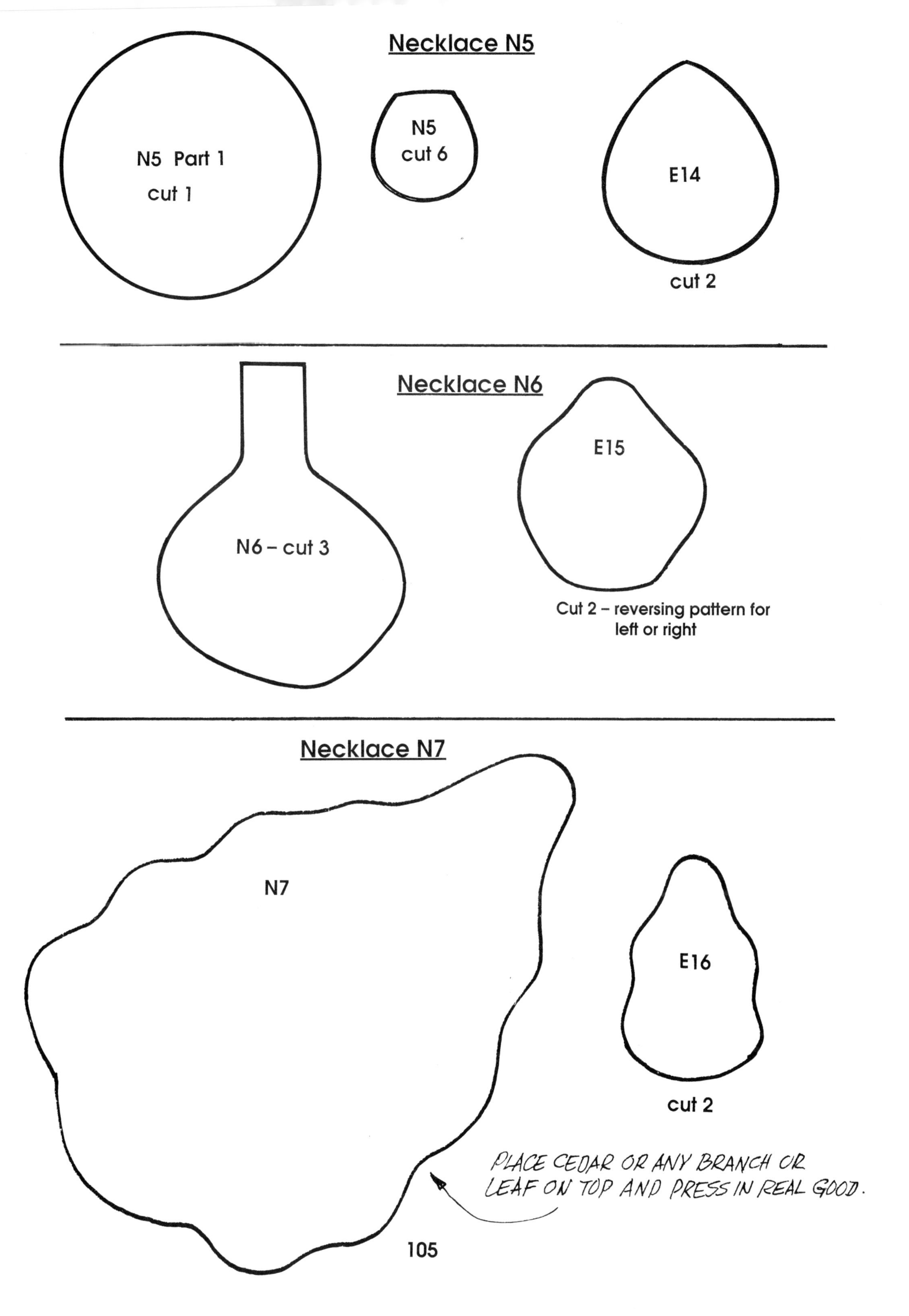
Necklace N5
N5 Part 1
cut 1
N5
cut 6
E14
cut 2
Necklace N6
N6 – cut 3
E15
Cut 2 – reversing pattern for
left or right
Necklace N7
N7
E16
cut 2
PLACE CEDAR OR ANY BRANCH OR
LEAF ON TOP AND PRESS IN REAL GOOD.

Necklace N8

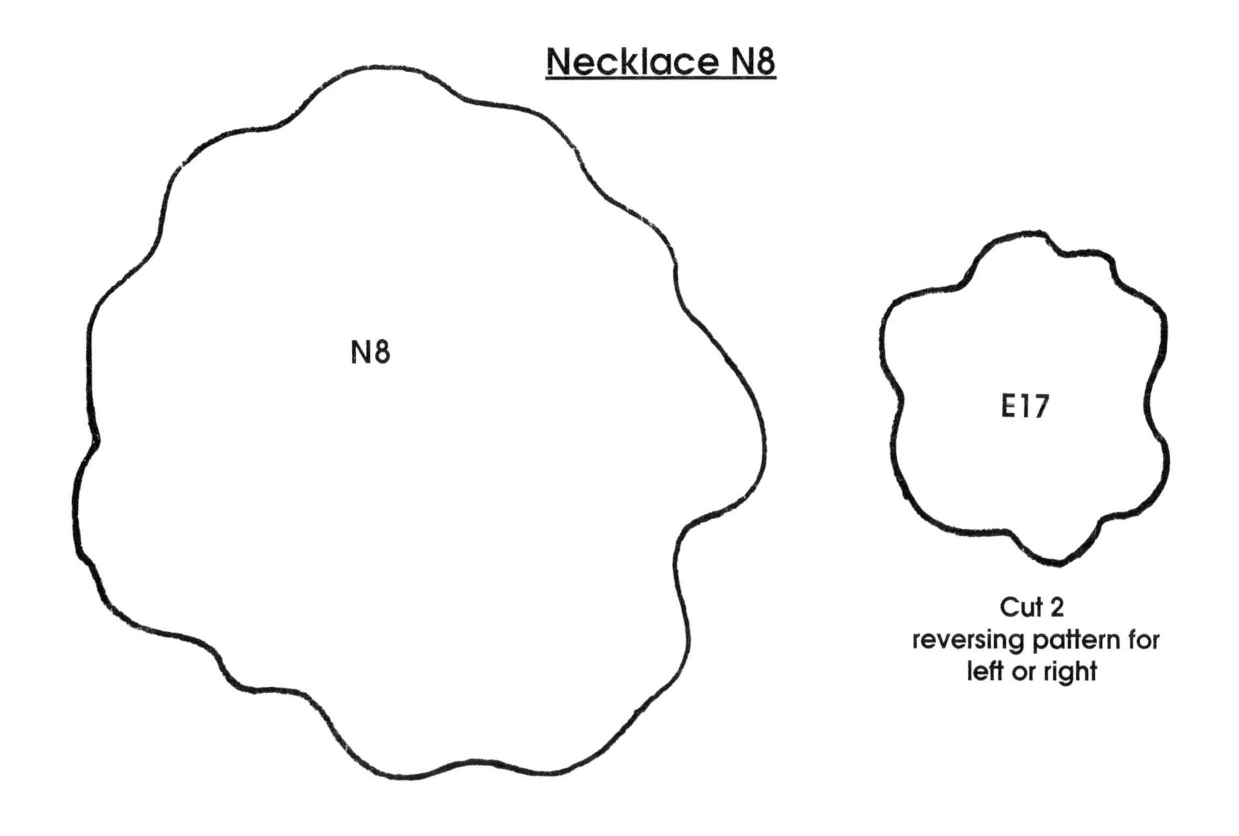

Necklace N9

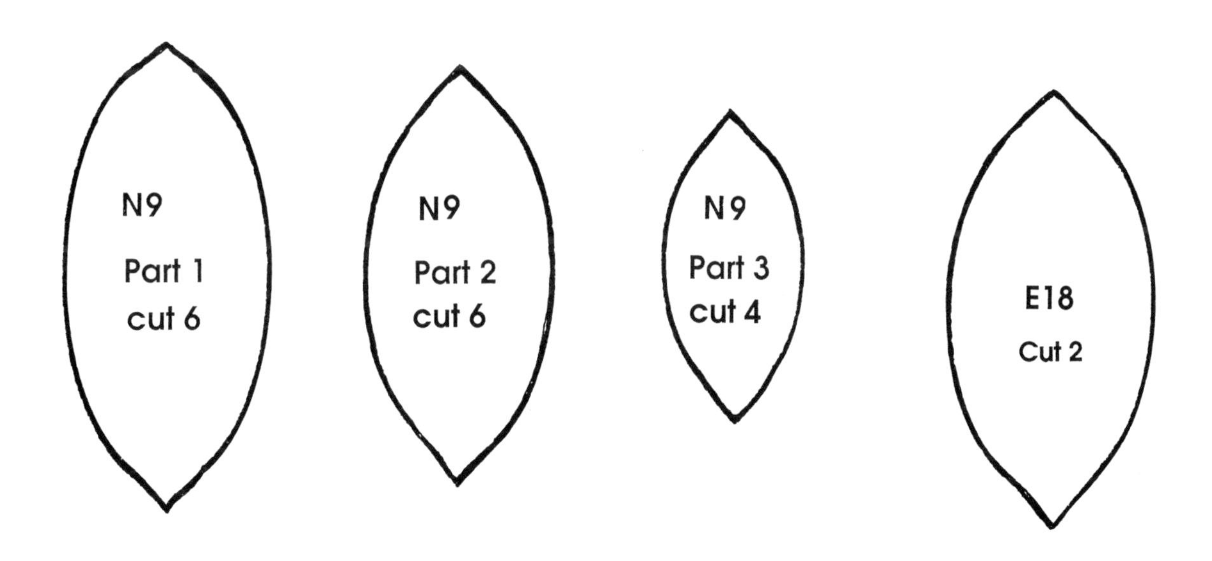

Necklace N10

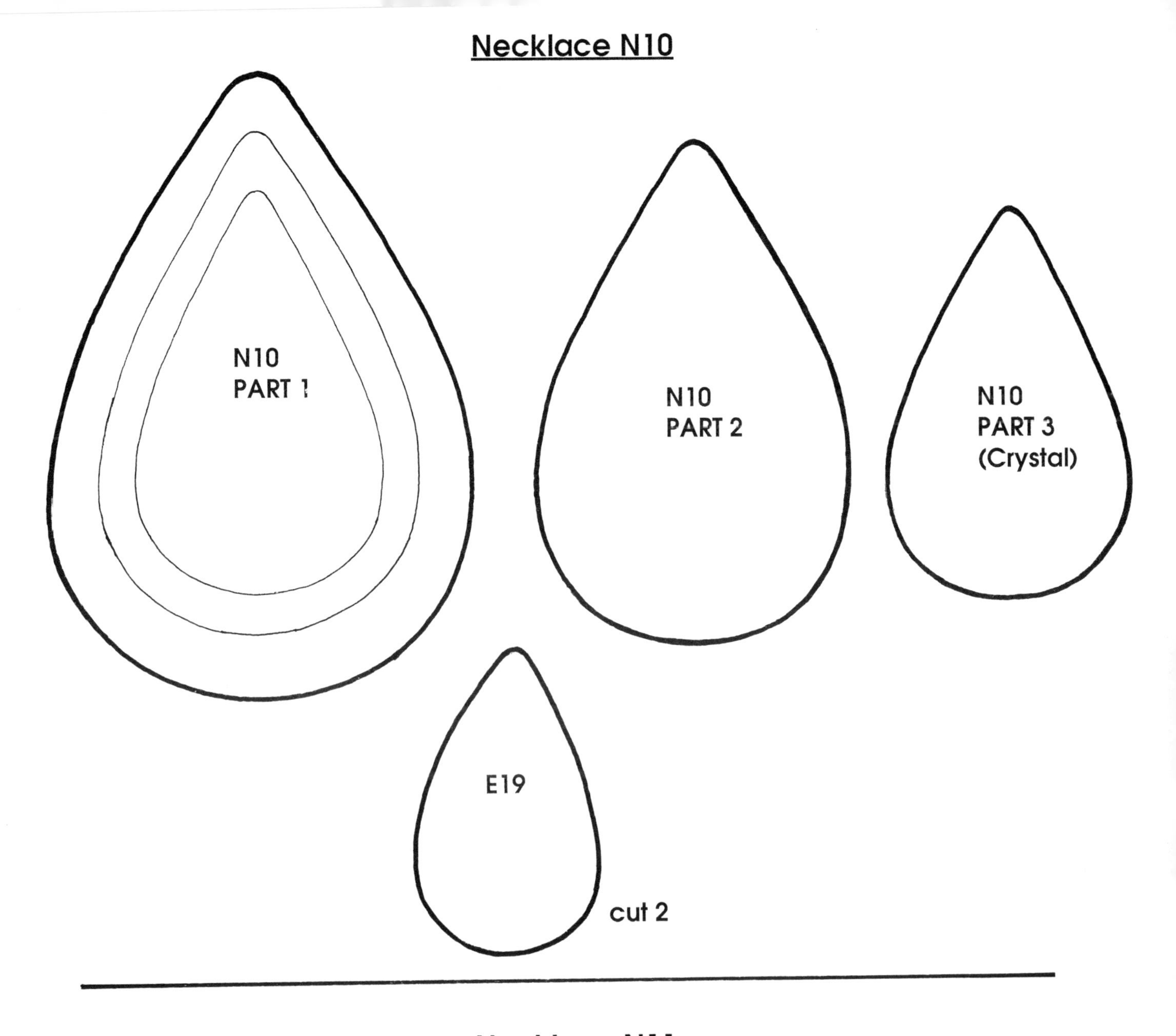

Necklace N11

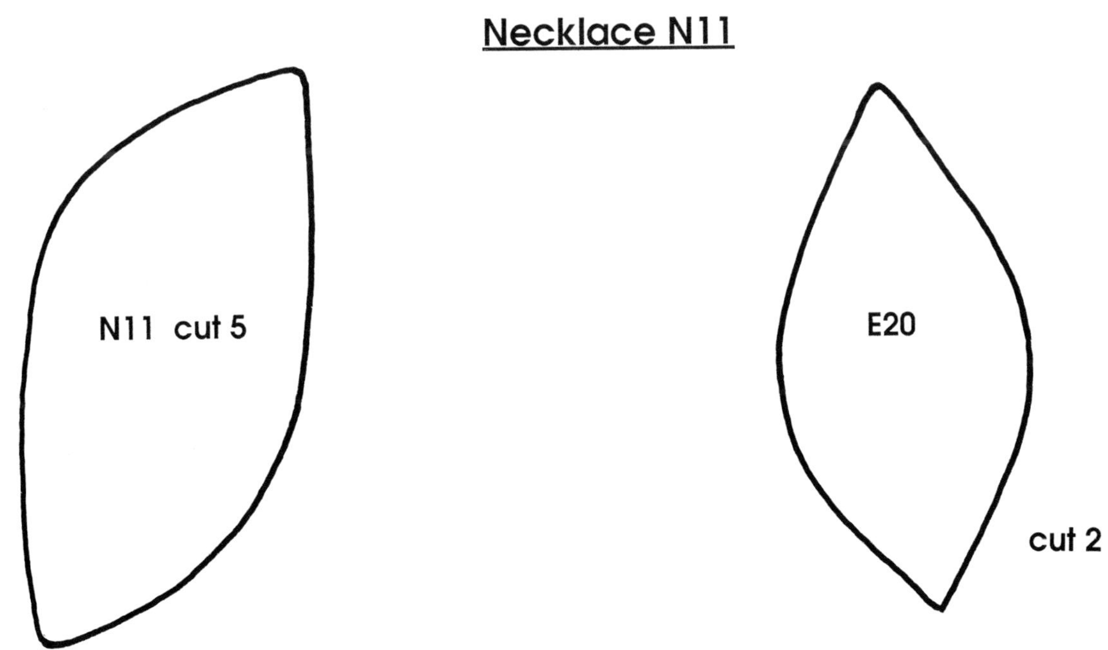

Contributing Designers

Designing and creating has been a way of life for Suzanne Kaiser. She left the teaching profession to pursue her very versatle design abilities. She designed a line of handwoven clothing that developed into a successful business. To complete these creations she made belts, buttons and jewelry to compliment each outfit. These were made from porcelain, yarns, paper and more recently from oven-fired modeling compound.

She is also an avid horticulturist and garden designer. The colors and forms in these gardens are more often than not the source of inspiration for her work. We're very fortunate to have a designer of Suzanne's caliber included in this book.

Knowing Cathy Behr's background in art and design we are very happy that she has agreed to share some of her work with us. She is a very talented painter, using techniques she developed with acrylics, collage and air brush.

The students in her private art classes are taught all forms of art, including paper making, clay drawing, painting, charcoal drawing to name a few. She is presently involved in creating exciting jewelry pieces from oven-fired modeling compound. Her one-of-a-kind designs are much in demand.

The Designer/Author

Betty Foster's formal education was in interior design but later she found working in clay much more rewarding. A twenty-five year career designing and selling porcelain and stoneware pottery, wall-hangings and jewelry enables her to share her designs and techniques in oven-fired modeling compound – her latest venture – as well as in ceramics.

She has been working with this modeling compound for some time now and is fascinated with the numerous ways it can be used. Her designs from this remarkable material are being sold in shops along with her ceramic pieces.